A PUBLICATION OF THE
HORACE MANN–LINCOLN INSTITUTE OF SCHOOL EXPERIMENTATION
TEACHERS COLLEGE, COLUMBIA UNIVERSITY

TALENTED YOUTH PROJECT MONOGRAPH

ADOLESCENT ATTITUDES

TOWARD

ACADEMIC BRILLIANCE

BY

ABRAHAM J. TANNENBAUM

ASSOCIATE DEAN, GRADUATE SCHOOL OF EDUCATION
YESHIVA UNIVERSITY

TALENTED YOUTH PROJECT MONOGRAPH

BUREAU OF PUBLICATIONS
TEACHERS COLLEGE, COLUMBIA UNIVERSITY
NEW YORK, 1962

Preface

For nearly ten years, there has been a resurgence of public interest in intellectual excellence in the schools. To the adult, the import has seemed clear. The education of the talented high school student must be improved. One might ask, how do the high school students—the objects of much of this concern—feel about it?

Dr. Tannenbaum has given a responsible and detailed answer in this research. If the answer of our youth is not what we would have hoped, at least we have here a thoroughgoing statement of it. If the youth have a business-as-usual outlook, perhaps they are reflecting the adult world as it is, not as the adults talk about it.

This contribution to the general national conversation on the education of the academically talented is the most recent in a series from the Talented Youth Project of the Horace Mann–Lincoln Institute of School Experimentation. This Project was organized in the early 1950's, when the great population increase was just appearing in the elementary schools, and it was clear that the able students in the high schools might suffer because so much attention was being diverted to the purely economic problems of housing and finance.

Since then, the educational times have changed—at least, for the adults. Perhaps our next task is even more difficult—to convince our youth of our sincerity with respect to the importance of intellectual pursuits. Perhaps it is the most difficult of all—to influence their social values in a way that supports what is validly intellectual about the high school curriculum. For, as Dr. Tannenbaum's study implies, in the degree that we fail them in this crucial field, they fail themselves.

ARTHUR W. FOSHAY
Executive Officer

DEDICATED

To my beloved, departed brother, Morris

May the tenderness and human decency
He inspired
In all who knew him
Be his everlasting monument.

Acknowledgments

I find it impossible to set down in words the depth of my gratitude to those who helped bring this study to completion. Nor does space permit mention of more than a few of the people who can justifiably regard the project as partly their own even though they are not answerable for its imperfections.

Professor Goodwin Watson provided early encouragement, recognizing that such an inquiry could be vitally meaningful to those concerned about the status of academic endeavor among adolescents. When the investigation was completed, he strongly urged a wide dissemination of its outcomes.

To the late Professor Irving Lorge goes the major credit for helping create the over-all research design. His brilliant counsel was offered willingly and abundantly throughout the project, not only on fundamental matters but on intricate details as well. Professor Robert L. Thorndike made key contributions to methodology and served as a sounding board for problems occurring every step of the way.

As director of the Talented Youth Project of the Horace Mann–Lincoln Institute of School Experimentation, Professor A. Harry Passow included this inquiry among the series of investigations for which he assumed supervisory responsibility. He extended to me the opportunity, guidance, and friendship that not only made the study possible but also contributed immeasurably to my personal and professional growth.

I want to express also my deepest gratitude to Professor Miriam L. Goldberg for her long and patient counsel throughout the study. As research associate with the Talented Youth Project, she identified herself as closely with the study as if it were her very own and provided penetrating criticism that was indispensable to my work.

Finally, my wife Annette served as the kind of helpmate that only a truly devoted wife can be. Without her inspiration and help this manuscript would surely have been stillborn.

ABRAHAM J. TANNENBAUM

Contents

PREFACE, BY ARTHUR W. FOSHAY   v

1. INTRODUCTION   1

2. ADOLESCENT ATTITUDES TOWARD LEARNING AND THE LEARNED   5
   VERBAL STEREOTYPES   6
   FACE-TO-FACE ATTITUDES   9
   THE NEED FOR ADDITIONAL EVIDENCE   12
       Adolescent Attitudes toward Academic Brilliance   12
       In the Context of Effort at School   13
       In the Context of Sports-mindedness   14
       Possible Background Influences on Attitudes   16
   SUMMARY   18

3. TECHNIQUES FOR ASSESSING ADOLESCENT ATTITUDES   20
   INSTRUMENTATION OF THE STUDY   21
       Background for Designing the Instrument   21
       Construction of the Instrument   23
       Scoring Procedures   28
       Plan for Administering the Instrument   29
       Reliability of the Instrument   30
       Intercorrelations among Character Scores   30
   POPULATION TESTED   31
   BACKGROUND INFORMATION ON STUDENTS AND THEIR PARENTS   32
       Parents' Education   32
       Scholastic Ability   32
   DATA ANALYSIS PROCEDURES   33
       Statistical Approach   33
       Qualitative Analysis   33
       Background Factors   34

4. ADOLESCENT REACTIONS TO ACADEMIC BRILLIANCE   35
   HOW THE STIMULUS CHARACTERS WERE RATED   35

RATINGS OF CHARACTERISTICS SINGLY AND IN COMBINATION   38

EVIDENCE FROM OTHER SCHOOLS   42

INTERPRETATION OF ATTITUDES   43

Reactions to Academic Ability   46

Reactions to Effort at School and Athleticism   49

TRAITS TYPIFYING THE CHARACTERS   51

Global Scores and Ratings on Special Traits   52

Differences in Trait Associations among Characters   53

Designation of Stimulus Character as "Boy," "Girl," or "Either"   57

RELATIONSHIP BETWEEN BACKGROUND FACTORS AND ATTITUDES   58

RELATIONS OF MALES AND FEMALES   60

RATINGS OF CHARACTERISTICS SINGLY AND IN COMBINATION   62

INTERPRETATION OF DISAGREEMENTS BETWEEN THE SEXES   66

SUMMARY OF OUTCOMES AND CONCLUSIONS   68

5. POSTSCRIPT ON IMPLICATIONS   69

VERBAL STEREOTYPES AS INDICES OF ATTITUDES   69

The Meaning of Global Score   69

Implications for Predicting Face-to-face Relationships   71

IMPLICATIONS FOR EDUCATIONAL POLICY AND RESEARCH   74

APPENDIX A: TRAIT CLUSTERS CONTAINING ADJECTIVES AND DESCRIPTIVE PHRASES   81

APPENDIX B: ATTITUDE QUESTIONNAIRE   83

APPENDIX C: STATISTICAL ANALYSES OF STUDENT REACTIONS   93

ADOLESCENT ATTITUDES

TOWARD

ACADEMIC BRILLIANCE

I

Introduction

One of the paramount concerns of America today is the development of youth talented in the arts, sciences, and humanities. Recent years have witnessed a veritable deluge of spoken and published words exhorting schools to step up their efforts at identifying and nurturing extraordinary young talent. Hardly a newspaper reader, radio listener or television viewer has failed to receive some message on the crucial role of brain-power in the nation's welfare and the importance of training gifted young minds to advance the frontiers of knowledge. Symptomatic of this up-surging popular interest is French's[1] finding that the number of articles on the gifted written from 1956 through 1958 exceeded the accumulated writings on this subject of the preceding three decades.

Basically, there is sound reason behind a free society's desire to culti-vate the talents of its ablest youth. Democracy thrives on a rich and abundant flowering of ideas. It champions the uniqueness of the individ-ual, however extraordinary he may be, and obliges the masses to support him in his struggle toward self-realization. It believes likewise in the power and worth of the masses, and encourages the talented person to serve them as best he can by contributing nobly to their cultural treasures. These are the principal considerations that make the pursuit of excellence part and parcel of the American tradition.

In recent years, however, developments in the world's political arena have tinged the spirit of our talent search with a note of alarm. Ever since Sputnik I was hurled into orbit, national pride in several time-honored institutions has been shaken severely. Hitherto complacent Americans have been panicked by threats to our worldwide leadership in technology and, by implication, the supremacy of our educational system in producing trail-blazing scientists and engineers. For some, the initial shock led to disenchantment with the nation's schools, which in turn brought on the

[1] J. L. French (ed.), *Educating the Gifted* (New York: Henry Holt & Company, 1959).

1

inevitable cries for reform. Others, less jittery, have taken a broader view of the problem and recognize it for what it really is, namely, a sign of the total ideological warfare being waged today, which brings into the contest a nation's scientific, artistic, and intellectual resources to propagate its way of life. Most Americans have been jolted into awareness of the fact that a cultural offensive can be as potent as a military assault. They are coming to realize that cold-war battles are won by sponsorship of world-wide concert tours by native artists, by announcements of scientific discoveries and unprecedented technological feats, by dazzling exhibitions at industrial fairs, and even by victories at the Olympic Games.

Mobilization of America's brainpower has consequently become a prime desideratum in the second half of the twentieth century, and its success may be the key to the nation's future. Responsible citizens proclaim that "at a time when we face problems of desperate gravity and complexity an undiscovered talent, a wasted skill, a misapplied ability, is a threat to the capacity of a free people to survive."[2] Public officials also regard talent development as a vital part of a program for national survival in an era when hostile political systems are making it clear to the world that knowledge is power and that the fruits of erudition and creativity can be used to beguile or intimidate people everywhere. Evidence of America's political investment in the talented is reflected in the recent decision by Congress to grant financial aid to the identification and guidance of able students under a national defense education act.[3] Even the title[4] of this piece of legislation shows that men in public office regard the school's task of enlarging the nation's talent reservoir as crucial to national survival.

Aside from the general shock effect of current pleas for excellence, there can be no gainsaying their impact on the learning aspirations of the gifted. Many able youth, who might otherwise face the educational challenge with indifference, probably feel compelled by the sonority and import of these appeals to make full and purposeful use of their innate capacities. For today's brainpower quest carries with it not only the promise of improved school provisions for superior students, but of greater social rewards as well. It stands to reason that public prestige would be

[2] Rockefeller Brothers Fund, Inc., *The Pursuit of Excellence and the Future of America;* Panel Report V of the Special Studies Project (Garden City, New York: Doubleday & Company, 1958), p. v.

[3] National Defense Education Act of 1958. Public Law 85-864, 85th Congress, H.R. 13247, September 2, 1958. (Washington, D.C.: U.S. Laws and Statutes, etc.), p. 1.

[4] The title page defines this law as "An act to strengthen the national defense and assist in the expansion and improvement of educational programs to meet critical national needs . . ."

conferred upon those capable of responding to a stirring popular demand.

Considering, therefore, the climate of urgency in which talent is being sought, and despite the resultant likelihood of a growing respect for the gifted in this country, there is serious need to determine whether mental superiority enhances or blemishes the social status of its possessor. What are the gains or risks involved in earning a reputation as being "brilliant," or "talented," or "a brain"? Although advanced training can probably earn more admiration and honor for the able person today than ever before, this does not imply that it contributes to his *personal* popularity as well. Social stature and social acceptance do not necessarily go together; indeed, respect for learning may often be coupled with disdain of the learned.

Needed, then, is a clear assessment of the desirability of intellectual pursuits as viewed by American youth. In deciding upon a "life of the mind," it is not enough for the gifted student to be aware of his crucial mission in an era of national emergency. He must also feel secure in his relationship with peers and know that he will not be stigmatized by them for his academic attainments. Little imagination is required to visualize the effects of apathy and resentment of schoolmates on the talented youth's will to excel. There is an all-too-familiar ring to the words of a high school student ranked in the highest decile in intelligence and scholastic aptitude who replied as follows when asked to explain his near-failing grades:

Well, some kids study all the time . . . but the class usually doesn't like them . . . Well, there's one kid who was in our school last year—he was a brain in mathematics and he knew what the Einstein theory was. He couldn't play baseball or anything like that, but when he got to school he studied and got a hundred in every subject. When he got home, he got right to his homework and started studying and went to bed at eleven. He doesn't have any physical life—you have to have physical and mental [life] to keep well. That guy didn't have many friends . . . Other kids practically made fun of him . . . If I really wanted to, I could get one of the highest marks in the class, but if I did that I wouldn't have very many friends and I think friends are important, too.[5]

Recognizable though these sentiments may be, there is little empirical evidence to indicate whether or not they are widespread in and out of the school world. Certainly, not enough empirical research is available to suggest meaningful hypotheses regarding America's attitudes toward the intellectual. Most of the writings on the subject are purely judgmental. As Gordon states,

[5] Jane Beasley, "Summary of Interviews: DeWitt Clinton Tenth Graders" (New York: Horace Mann–Lincoln Institute of School Experimentation, Teachers College, Columbia University, 1956–1957), p. 12 (mimeographed).

In the face of a dearth of empirical research dealing specifically with the position of intellectuals in the American social structure, consideration of the topic must rely at present on general observation, occasional impressionistic essays by sociologists and litterateurs alike, and inferences made from research on related materials.[6]

Noteworthy, however, are the conclusions drawn in much of the expounded theory referred to by Gordon, namely, that in this country the man of thought is rendered a social pariah in a variety of ways. Occasionally, he is regarded by his fellow men as a deviant, or even an eccentric, who "acts peculiar" through his refusal to accept their values and behavior;[7] often, he is feared as a dangerous radical, promoting the overthrow of popular social and political doctrines;[8] by some he is viewed as a lazy ivory-tower dweller who sometimes has the temerity to meddle in the affairs of the "hard-working folk;"[9] or, he may be belittled as a high priest of the "cult of the rational" who mistakenly believes man can control his destiny through guidance from his mental powers.[10]

How prevalent these attitudes are in society at large is not known, although the need for such understanding is especially vital at a time when the nation is endeavoring to mobilize its best brains in order that it may survive and prosper culturally. Nor does there exist a clear picture of the value attached to giftedness as a personal attribute by high school youth whose opinions, in the last analysis, may be crucial in determining the success of this mobilization effort.

In view of the importance of understanding more fully the attitudes toward academic brilliance in America, the present study addressed itself to this task. It attempted (1) to explore and systematize selected thoughts on the status of intellect in the adolescent world; (2) to obtain new empirical evidence on adolescent attitudes toward academic brilliance; and (3) to identify some possible influences on these attitudes.

[6] M. Gordon, "Social Class and American Intellectuals," *American Association of University Professors Bulletin,* Vol. 40, No. 4 (Winter 1954–1955), pp. 517–528.

[7] N. D. M. Hirsch, *Genius and Creative Intelligence* (Cambridge, Massachusetts: Sci-Art Publishers, 1931).

[8] S. S. Sargent and T. Brameld (eds.), "Anti-intellectualism in the United States," *Journal of Social Issues,* Vol. 40, No. 3 (1955), entire issue.

[9] M. E. Curti, *American Paradox* (Brunswick, New Jersey: Rutgers University Press, 1956).

[10] See C. Brinton, *The Shaping of the Modern Mind* (New York: New American Library of World Literature, 1953); and W. Barrett, *Irrational Man* (Garden City, New York: Doubleday & Company, 1958).

2

Adolescent Attitudes toward
Learning and the Learned

The question of how Americans, in general, perceive intellectuals has not as yet been subjected to rigorous study. The need for such investigation, of course, is self-evident. A nation alerted to the pursuit of excellence must examine carefully the nature of public opinion concerning its most creative minds. For if the social climate discourages mental development beyond a certain point there is danger that highest-level intellectual endeavors will be undertaken only by those gifted people—preciously few as they are—who seem willing to risk social rejection.

Brameld[1] points out that where anti-intellectualism permeates social and political life in America it is likely to penetrate the schools as well. These attitudes can cripple incentives toward achievement among high school students who are at a stage of development when they reach crucial decisions about their academic future. To the extent that peer group attitudes affect such decisions, it becomes important to examine how highly the adolescent subculture in America values academic brilliance. The problem is further dramatized by what is known about the powerful pressures among adolescents to conform to group traditions and values. Teenagers live in a kind of twilight world between childhood and adulthood and are often forced to establish a subculture that can "set itself off as recognizably distinct and separate from the adult society which refuses it membership."[2] In confronting the adult world with their own demands and in resisting the pressures of adult authority, youth must present a united front with a minimum of deviations among individual members. Moreover, as Ausubel points out,

[1] T. Brameld, "Anti-Intellectualism in Education," *Journal of Social Issues,* Vol. 40, No. 3 (1955), pp. 35–40.
[2] D. P. Ausubel, *Theory and Problems of Adolescent Development* (New York: Grune & Stratton, 1954), p. 354.

Adolescents are partly *motivated* to perceive age mates as deviants, non-conformists, and out-groupers because by doing so they can enhance the value of their own conformity and in-group status. The larger the number of persons who can be perceived as *outside* the charmed circle, the more individuals they can perceive as inferior to themselves, the greater their own self-esteem becomes by comparison, and the more status value their in-group membership acquires.[3]

With pressures toward conformity so pronounced among adolescents—more, perhaps than among adults—one would expect to find them highly sensitized to the behavior expectations of the group, and disciplined accordingly. And if being dubbed a "brain," a "genius," or an "egg-head" implies censure by the adolescent subculture in America, it is conceivable that the highly gifted high school student may often feel pressured to mask his intellectual abilities in order to attain group acceptance.

Just as there is little research to reveal much about the status of the intellectual in adult society, there are also few studies that can lead to judgments about the place of academic excellence in the adolescent value system and the social position of the scholarly among their teen-age peers. What empirical evidence there is often derives from investigations which focus only obliquely on the subject. But even direct investigations vary with regard to definition of giftedness and social status as well as in their methodology to such an extent that definite conclusions are not possible.

VERBAL STEREOTYPES

One clue to the adolescent attitudes toward schooling may be found in a 1953 study by Remmers and Radler.[4] They reported that fully 75 to 80 per cent of a nationwide sample of high school students reported liking school, but only 14 per cent viewed acquiring an "academic background" as "the most important thing young people should get out of high school." The majority (72 per cent) called "knowing how to get along with people," "understanding our society," "acquiring a sense of discipline and responsibility" the real goals of high school education; another 14 per cent rated "vocational skills" first. In part, these findings agree with Roper's 1950[5] survey of the adult population, in which only 13 per cent nominated the development of an "academic background" as an important objective

[3] *Ibid.,* p. 355.
[4] H. H. Remmers and D. H. Radler, *The American Teenager* (Indianapolis: Bobbs-Merrill Company, 1957).
[5] Reported in Remmers and Radler, *op. cit.*

for the American student. Both studies lend support to the observations made by Laski and Lerner, that education for scholastic excellence seems less important than training for social competence in this country.

A direct investigation by the Gilbert Youth Research[6] of adolescent attitudes toward "eggheads" found that fully two thirds of the young people questioned defined this term as "a very intellectual person" and regarded the appellation an insult. Gilbert noted that adolescents distinguish sharply between the "egghead" and an "educated person." As one of his subjects remarked: "I am going to college not because I expect to spend the rest of my life in a library but because I think college prepares us to understand not only books but nature and people and, most of all, to enjoy life more." This is further evidence that teen-agers do not view the acquisition of an academic background as the most important goal of secondary education.

A more recent study reported by Coleman is directly relevant to the attitudes of teen-agers toward academic outstandingness. He asked a group of boys from several high schools to answer the question, "How would you most like to be remembered in school: as an athletic star, a brilliant student, or most popular?" Results showed a tendency to select "star athlete" over either of the other choices. The boys were then asked to indicate which of the three descriptions most typified members of the leading crowd in school, and again the responses were directed away from the ideal of the brilliant student. Asked to respond to a similar questionnaire—but with "brilliant student," "leader in extracurricular activities," and "most popular" as the trio of choices—a group of adolescent girls likewise tended to select "brilliant student" less often than the others. Most important, Coleman found a direct relationship between the frequency with which each of several school populations mentioned "good grades" as a means of getting into the leading crowd and the degree to which the average IQs of the straight "A" students exceeded the mean IQs for the total student body in the respective schools. According to Coleman,

The implications for American society as a whole are clear. Because high schools allow the adolescent sub-cultures to divert energies into athletics, social activities, and the like, they recruit into intellectual activities people with a rather mediocre level of ability.[7]

[6] E. Gilbert, " 'Egghead' to Them Is an Insult," Philadelphia *Inquirer,* July 25, 1958.

[7] J. S. Coleman, "The Adolescent Subculture and Academic Achievement," *American Journal of Sociology,* Vol. 65 (January 1960), pp. 337–347.

Further clues to adolescent attitudes toward academic endeavor and success come from unpublished interviews[8] of high school students who scored above IQ 125 and were at least two years accelerated in basic skills as measured by standardized tests, but were achieving below expectation at school. One boy stated, "I'm average, a little above average. I think the ones who are geniuses . . . they are bookworms. Too much. They don't do anything after school. They don't participate in activities or anything. They just study, and I don't want to be like them." Another underachiever remarked, "Being in Special Progress Classes [for gifted students] didn't make any difference [in popularity]. It was how you could play baseball or something—it didn't matter how smart you were. Kids who were not good at sports usually made it up at social activities."

In a major study of the social system of a high school, Gordon examined the contribution of academic standing to general status which he defined as a

. . . composite of separate positions held in the three sub-systems of school organization: (1) The formal organization of the school which prescribes learning achievement; (2) the system of student organizations usually referred to as extra-curricular activities; and (3) the network of interpersonal relationships defined by friendship choices.[9]

He found that grade achievement was less significantly related to general status than either club participation or sociometric rating. The boys conferred greatest prestige on the athlete and on a social type called the "big wheel" who combines such attributes as athletic prowess and conformity to approved patterns of dress, dating, and recreational pursuits. The girls polarized their prestige choices around the position of Yearbook Queen, whose choice was based on certain habits of dress, school service, democratic personality, leadership ability, and puritan morals. Thus, achievement in student activities rather than scholastic attainment was most significantly related to a favorable social position for both boys and girls. It was found, too, that at least five major cliques were formed in this school and they could be differentiated as follows in the rank order of their influence among peers: (1) the athletic crowd; (2) the music and club activity crowd; (3) the dating crowd; (4) the "brainy" crowd; and (5) the hunting and fishing crowd. Here again, the "brains" were rated relatively low, this time as opinion leaders.

[8] Jane Beasley, "Summary of Interviews: DeWitt Clinton Tenth Graders" (New York: Horace Mann–Lincoln Institute of School Experimentation, Teachers College, Columbia University, 1956–1957; mimeographed).

[9] C. W. Gordon, *The Social System of the High School: A Study in the Sociology of Adolescence* (Glencoe, Illinois: Free Press, 1957), p. 3.

Two large-scale investigations of adolescents' attitudes toward the scientist are noteworthy for the conflicting results they produced. In one study by Mead and Metraux,[10] some 35,000 high school students revealed ambivalent feelings in their responses to a questionnaire on their perceptions of scientists. Although the "official" image of the scientist, independent of personal involvement by the respondent, was a positive one, the image was likely to invoke negative verbal stereotypes when science was thought of as a career choice or when scientists were considered in terms of possible marriage partners. While conceding the prestige of science as a profession, teen-agers felt that the intellectual activity involved is unrewarding and lures one away from normal, friendly relationships with human beings.

However, Allen's[11] study of teen-agers' attitudes toward science and scientific careers produced seemingly different reactions. Of the 3,057 high school seniors responding to an attitudes scale, 73 per cent disagreed and 7 per cent agreed with such statements as, "Scientists are communistic." "Scientists often have physical deformities which render them unfit for other work." "Scientists are usually unsociable." The remaining 20 per cent of the responses were either neutral or omitted.

FACE-TO-FACE ATTITUDES

Assessments of gifted students' status in face-to-face associations with peers suggest that they generally fare well in comparison to the less able. There is also evidence that points to a curvilinear relationship between intelligence and social status. Up to a certain level on the intelligence continuum, as measured by tests of mental ability, the correlation is positive, but beyond that point the relationship apparently breaks down.

Terman's studies of the social status of gifted children and youth indicate that they compare favorably with the nongifted.[12] When questioned, "Is the child considered by others as 'queer' or different? If so, in what way?" 12 per cent of the teachers' responses regarding the gifted boys were in the affirmative, as against 5 per cent for the boys in the control group. With respect to the girls, 7 per cent of the teachers' responses were

[10] Margaret Mead and Rhoda Metraux, "The Image of the Scientist Among High School Students: A Pilot Study," *Science*, August 30, 1957.

[11] H. Allen, Jr., *Attitudes of Certain High School Seniors Toward Science and Scientific Careers* (New York: Bureau of Publications, Teachers College, Columbia University, 1959).

[12] L. M. Terman and others, *Mental and Physical Traits of a Thousand Gifted Children: Genetic Studies of Genius,* Vol. I (Stanford, California: Stanford University Press, 1926).

"yes" for the gifted, as compared to 5 per cent for the controls. Ten per cent of the parents of the gifted boys answered "yes" to the same question; 8 per cent did likewise for the girls. When these able children grew to adolescence,[13] the same question was asked of the parents and the responses were similar to their earlier ones. Terman also found little difference in the extent to which the companionship of gifted as compared to control children was sought by peers.[14]

Nevertheless, social adjustment ratings on twenty-five of the most highly gifted children in Terman's population revealed problems not found among the moderately gifted. None of those with IQ 170 and above rated among the highest in social adjustment, whereas the proportion of those rated lowest was about twice that of the total gifted group.[15] Terman's staff concluded from these results "that the child of 180 IQ has one of the most difficult jobs of social adjustment that any human being is ever called upon to meet."[16] Similar conclusions were drawn from other studies, notably those done by Hollingworth[17] in the New York City schools, and by Zorbaugh and associates[18] at the New York University Counseling Center for Gifted Children. The latter studies include one in a large city high school where the highly gifted were found to be well below average in extracurricular participation at school and were also failing in their attempts to relate well to adult groups.

A study of sociometric ratings of gifted junior high school students in the Toronto secondary schools,[19] found that up to IQ 150, the higher the intelligence quotient the greater the likelihood of achieving high social standing. The number of cases with IQs above 150 was too small to warrant further study of the linear relationship between social acceptance and intelligence, but the tendency was for the status ratings to drop beyond this IQ level. Miller[20] likewise discovered a positive correlation up

[13] Barbara Burks, Dortha Jensen, and L. M. Terman, *The Promise of Youth: Genetic Studies of Genius,* Vol. III (Stanford, California: Stanford University Press, 1930).

[14] Terman and others, *op. cit.*

[15] Burks, Jensen, and Terman, *op. cit.*

[16] *Ibid.,* p. 265.

[17] Leta S. Hollingworth, *Children Above 180 I.Q.: Origin and Development* (Yonkers, New York: World Book Company, 1942).

[18] H. Zorbaugh, Rhea K. Boardman, and P. Sheldon, "Some Observations of Highly Gifted Children," in P. Witty (ed.), *The Gifted Child* (Boston: D. C. Heath & Company, 1951), Chapter 5.

[19] Association of Heads of Guidance Departments, Research Committee, *A Study of Thirty-two Gifted Students of the Toronto Secondary Schools* (Toronto, Canada: Toronto Secondary Schools, 1955).

[20] R. B. Miller, "Social Status and Socioempathic Differences among Mentally Superior, Mentally Typical, and Mentally Retarded Children," *Exceptional Child,* Vol. 23 (December 1956), pp. 114–119.

to certain limits of the intellectual continuum between social status and intelligence. He concluded, however, that high social status is conferred on the gifted, not because of their intelligence but because of certain personality traits they seem capable of acquiring with greater ease than do the nongifted. In a laboratory school, where students of average intelligence rank in the highest decile in scholastic achievement according to national norms, it was found that the high achievers of the seventh grade began to emerge as social leaders. Haggard observed that

... actually they were respected more than liked by their peers. The fact that the high academic achievers became the social leaders also suggests an important characteristic of the school's atmosphere, since in most classrooms these children would probably be snubbed as "grinds" and "bookworms." [21]

Other sociometric studies also show a positive relationship between academic and social status. Bonney[22] found that those elementary school children rating in the highest quartile in sociometric choice were intellectually superior to those of the lowest quartile. Grossman and Wrighter[23] tion on the elementary school level was reported by Williams[24] who found a positive correlation between academic performance and acceptance of and by the group, although the gifted children accepted the group more readily than they were accepted by it.

Even though most studies of the relationship between scholastic ability and social acceptance at school have been done in the elementary grades, the little evidence available on secondary school populations tends to show that the positive correlation is sustained even in these older groups. Nason's[25] study of above-average high school students reveals that the high achievers among the intellectually gifted attain better social status with peers than do the equally able low achievers. In a survey of several hundred students in a suburban senior high school, more than two thirds

[21] E. A. Haggard. "Socialization, Personality, and Academic Achievement in Gifted Children," *School Review,* Vol. 65 (December 1957), pp. 388–414.

[22] M. E. Bonney, "Relationships Between Social Success, Family Size, Socioeconomic Background and Intelligence among School Children in Grades 3 to 5, *Sociometry,* Vol. 7 (1944), pp. 26–39.

[23] Beverly Grossman and Joyce Wrighter, "The Relationship between Selection-Rejection and Intelligence, Social Status, and Personality amongst Sixth Grade Children," *Sociometry,* Vol. 11 (1948), pp. 346–355.

obtained similar results in a study of sixth graders. Still another investiga-

[24] Meta F. Williams, "Acceptance and Performance among Gifted Elementary School Children," *Educational Research Bulletin,* Ohio State University, Vol. 37, No. 8 (November 12, 1958).

[25] L. J. Nason, *Academic Achievement of Gifted High School Students,* Southern California Educational Monograph No. 17 (Los Angeles: University of Southern California Press, 1958).

of whom were college-bound, Ryan and Davie[26] found a slight positive relationship between social acceptance and school grades, and an even slighter apparent relationship between social acceptance and scholastic aptitude as measured by the American Council on Education scores. According to the investigators, these findings cast doubt on the old supposition that social isolates turn to intensive school work for compensation.

THE NEED FOR ADDITIONAL EVIDENCE

Adolescent Attitudes toward Academic Brilliance . . .

In view of the dearth of evidence on teen-agers' attitudes toward their academically gifted peers, the present study attempted to explore such attitudes in some depth. Specifically, it compared verbal stereotypes ascribed by high school juniors to students known as "academically brilliant" as against those known to be "average" in school work. These attitudes were directed toward imaginary peers rather than real ones.

Unlike face-to-face encounters with live individuals through which a variety of facts and impressions may be gained, what is known about an imaginary character is contained only in his description. Consequently, it may be argued that reactions to him are governed exclusively by the given information. If such an assumption were valid, the present study would involve simply the noting of traits associated with a fictitious character described only as "academically brilliant" and comparing them with traits ascribed to another imagined character known only as "academically average." This approach, however, would neglect the possibility that the reactions are not to the stated attribute, in this case academic ability, but to other unstated, though implied, characteristics in combination with ability. For example, when asked to indicate whether or not brilliant high school students generally get much fun out of life, the answer may be "no" because the respondent feels that most brilliant students behave in some special way that leads to a rather dull life. Thus, the reaction is directed to an inferred characteristic rather than exclusively to the one stated. In reality, people may be forgiven or admired for their brilliance by adolescents provided they do not adopt accompanying behavior patterns that are unpopular. On the other hand, such behavior may render a person unpopular, regardless of whether he is academically average or brilliant.

In order, then, to make possible a more detailed and meaningful inter-

---

[26] F. J. Ryan and J. S. Davie, "Social Acceptance, Academic Achievement and Academic Aptitude among High School Students," *Journal of Educational Research*, Vol. 52, No. 3 (November 1958), pp. 101–106.

pretation of attitudes, each character was portrayed not only in terms of his ability but also in terms of other carefully selected characteristics; namely, the amount of effort he exerts on school work and the extent of his interest in sports. These modifying attributes were chosen because they, too, are said to bear deep significance among adolescents.

. . . in the Context of Effort at School . . .

Stimulus characteristics referring to *effort* (e.g., studious versus non-studious) were added in order to test Mead's contention that diligence, more than ability in a worthwhile area of endeavor, is seen as a virtue in American society. Success in our culture, she claims, is extolled only if achieved by those with modest ability who rise to the top by dint of courage, perseverance, and occasionally suffering. As a result, "there is in America today an appalling waste of first-rate talent, while the slightly superior people, just because they do have to work hard to get straight A's, are forgiven."[27] Where the road to attainment does not adhere to the Horatio Alger myth—where an individual with extraordinary capacity for learning and exceptional creative powers is able to outshine his peers with comparative ease—there is little recognition and encouragement. Instead, his success is attributed merely to luck, over which he has weak control and for which he deserves no credit.

Mead's belief that the school rewards studiousness over effortless superiority may be a reference to the strong, traditional influence of the Protestant ethic, or, as Laski called it, the "quintessence of a secularized puritanism"[28] in America. By this is meant that hard work, stick-to-itive-ness, and pulling oneself up by the bootstraps are regarded as supreme virtues leading to success. Lack of effort and application, on the other hand, are seen as defects of character that usually bring on failure, no matter how high the ability. As Strodtbeck points out, success in our culture, as defined by status mobility, is to some degree linked with striving for educational success, and these ambitions spring from America's belief in hard work and the perfectibility of man.[29]

Whether or not Mead is justified in counting diligence at school among the virtues of industriousness in general is a question worth exploring. It is not known whether teachers are actually more favorably disposed toward students who earn straight A's the hard way than toward those who

[27] Margaret Mead, "The Gifted Child in the American Culture of Today," *Journal of Teacher Education,* Vol. 5 (1954), p. 213.
[28] H. J. Laski, *The American Democracy* (New York: Viking Press, 1948), p. 42.
[29] F. L. Strodtbeck, "Family Interaction, Values and Achievement," in D. C. McClelland and others, *Talent and Society* (Princeton, New Jersey: D. Van Nostrand Company, 1958).

are nimble-minded and achieve high grades without much effort. Even if it were so, there would be no basis for drawing similar conclusions about the attitudes of adolescents. True, grit and determination seem to be valued by teen-agers, especially when demonstrated on the ball field or in the gymnasium. The young athlete who spends many practice hours on the basketball court is probably admired for his hard work by peers, especially if it leads to stardom or even modest success. However, conscientiousness at school is another matter. If the teen-ager sees the aims of education as largely nonscholastic, he may consider studiousness a distraction from the most important activities of school and the studious as deviates from the adolescent norm. Furthermore, working hard on school assignments may be a sign of compliance with the demands and expectations of teachers, who may take a more serious view of academic accomplishment at school than do the students. Teachers may also represent to adolescents a kind of adult authority against which rebellion is often justified. If studiousness is perceived as an undesirable attribute among teenagers, it is important to determine whether it is equally undesirable in brilliant as in average students.

A study cited by Getzels[30] reveals something about teen-agers' regard for hard work and self-direction. In this investigation the abler students tended to espouse what Getzels calls America's "traditional secular values" which champion individualism and the struggle for personal success. The less able students, on the other hand, favored so-called "emergent values" which temper individual aspirations with sensitivity to the will of the group. Earlier, Terman's staff had also found that his gifted group rated significantly higher than the controls on such volitional characteristics as "desire to excel," "conscientiousness," "perseverance," and "desire to know."[31]

. . . and in the Context of Sports-mindedness

A second characteristic chosen to modify ability was athleticism (e.g., athletic versus nonathletic). The purpose was to test the effects of a powerful status-influencing attribute on the students' reactions to the imaginary characters. The value of athletic interests among teen-agers has often been the subject of commentary by social critics. Particularly noteworthy are some of the comparisons made between adolescents' feel-

[30] R. Prince, "A Study of the Relationships between Individual Values and Administrative Effectiveness in the School Situation" (unpublished doctoral dissertation, University of Chicago, 1957), reported in J. W. Getzels, "The Acquisition of Values in School and Society," in F. S. Chase and H. A. Anderson (eds.), *The High School in a New Era* (Chicago: University of Chicago Press, 1958), pp. 147–161.

[31] Burks, Jensen, and Terman, *op. cit.*

ings about academic as against athletic interests. Laski noted that instead of intellectual distinction being most treasured in American schools, "the real title to importance belongs to the successful athlete."[32] Another observer, Geoffrey Gorer, likewise observed that

Athletes as a class are admired, envied, and privileged; they represent their school against its neighbors and rivals; and all the boys, at any rate, are meant to follow the fortune of their teams with the greatest enthusiasm and emotional involvement.[33]

By way of contrast,

Scholastic achievement is one of the few spheres where American children are not pushed to the limit of their strength; compared with any country of western Europe, the standard required at any given age is low.[34]

Unlike the cases of stimulus characteristics referring to ability (e.g., academically brilliant versus average ability) and effort (e.g., studious versus nonstudious), ample research exists to determine the status of athleticism among teen-agers. There is no question about the athlete being one of the adolescent idols in this country. Olds[35] found that among 840 high school students, the boys listed sports above all preferred activities if there were more time and facilities. Biddulph's[36] study of 461 junior and senior high school boys revealed that those ranking high in athletic performance seemed to rate as better adjusted socially than those whose sports skills were mediocre. Drawing conclusions from previous research, Strang commented, "with boys, engaging in sports is an essential part of the growing process."[37] This seems to confirm Jones's[38] finding that competitive athletic skills are among the chief sources of social status in the period preceding maturity. Strang presented further noteworthy evidence that shows a higher percentage of gifted than nongifted students in junior high school demonstrating interest in sports, whereas the reverse

[32] Laski, *op. cit.,* p. 338.
[33] G. Gorer, "The All American Child," in B. N. Meltzer, H. R. Toby and P. M. Smith (eds.), *Education in Society: Readings* (New York: Thomas Y. Crowell Company, 1958), p. 54.
[34] *Ibid.,* p. 55.
[35] B. Olds, "How Do Young People Use Their Leisure Time?" *Recreation,* Vol. 42 (January 1949), pp. 458–463.
[36] L. G. Biddulph, "Athletic Achievement and the Personal and Social Adjustment of High School Boys," *Research Quarterly of the American Association for Health and Physical Education,* Vol. 25 (March 1954), pp. 1–7.
[37] Ruth Strang, *The Adolescent Views Himself* (New York: McGraw-Hill Book Company, 1957), p. 227.
[38] H. E. Jones, "Physical Ability as a Factor in Social Adjustment in Adolescence," *Journal of Educational Research,* Vol. 40 (December 1946), pp. 287–301.

is true in senior high school. She suggests the possibility that the older gifted students need more time to study in order to reach their goal and must therefore sacrifice some of the time they would normally devote to athletics.

In view of the known interests of American youth in sports, it would have seemed redundant to add athletic-mindedness (or the absence of it) to the description of each stimulus character in order merely to determine whether it enhances or detracts from the social acceptability of that character. On the contrary, however, athleticism was chosen deliberately *because* of its persuasive power. The purpose was to see the extent to which the known positive power of being athletic-minded would color attitudes toward those who possess the less acceptable characteristics of *ability* and *effort*. Is the social status of the teen-ager affected by being brilliant or average, studious or nonstudious, so long as he shows interest in sports? And, on the other hand, does the lack of interest in athletics derogate his status among schoolmates regardless of his achievement and diligence in class? Against the background of a strongly influential characteristic such as athleticism, much can be revealed about the place of academic ability and effort among adolescent values.

Possible Background Influences on Attitudes

An important aspect of this study was to ascertain how closely adolescents' own scholastic ability and socioeconomic status (as measured by the educational levels of their parents) correspond with their reactions to the hypothetical characters. It was hypothesized that the acceptability of academic brilliance would improve in direct relationship to the respondent's own academic status or to the level his parents had reached on the educational ladder. Students who are themselves intellectually superior should most readily regard this trait as desirable; and students whose parents show signs of highest respect for education by the number of years they have attended school should also be most accepting of mental excellence as a personal quality. Testing these suppositions empirically can shed light on the extent to which such background factors might help diversify attitudes in the adolescent world where conformity is expected.

Although research provides little information as to what influences attitudes toward learning and the learned, Hollingshead[39] suggests such factors as a student's academic ability as well as his experience in the family culture. Allen's study,[40] mentioned earlier, showed that the highly intelligent high school seniors were less apt to attach negative stereotypes

[39] A. B. Hollingshead, *Elmtown's Youth* (New York: John Wiley & Sons, 1949).
[40] Allen, *op. cit.*

to scientists than were their lower-ability classmates. In the matter of friendship choices, however, there seems to be some controversy about the relative attractability of gifted students to equally able peers. Gallagher's[41] study of 355 children in grades 2 to 5 revealed that although popularity is positively related to intellectual status, there is little sign of an unusual tendency for the bright children to choose comparably able classmates as friends. In Mann's study,[42] on the other hand, it was found that gifted and typical children are most likely to choose and reject those of their own group.

To the extent that motivation for college is an index of attitudes toward intellectual ability and preoccupation, there is evidence to suggest that the more able students have more accepting attitudes. Kahl's[43] studies of adolescents' educational aspirations show a positive correlation between IQ and the desire for a college education, even with fathers' occupational status held constant. Based on a sample of 3,348 boys in their sophomore and junior years in various high schools in the Boston metropolitan area, Kahl found that from the lowest to highest IQ quintile groups on each of five occupational levels, there was a steady rise in the percentage of respondents making plans for college.

The amount of parental education seems also to be associated with motivation for college attendance. Hyman[44] reported a survey on the differential emphasis on college education as expressed by some 3,000 adults who had reached various levels of schooling. He found that of those who had themselves attended college, 72 per cent recommended a college education, as compared to 55 per cent who had attended high schools and 36 per cent for those who had attended only grammar school. Noteworthy, too, is Kahl's finding that even in the lowest socioeconomic groups there was a greater tendency in favor of college among those boys whose parents valued college education as a means of social mobility than among boys whose parents attached relatively little importance to a college degree.[45]

From all indications, then, it was logical to hypothesize that the teen-

[41] J. J. Gallagher, "Peer Acceptance of Highly Gifted Children in Elementary School," *Elementary School Journal*, Vol. 58, No. 8 (May 1958), pp. 465–470.
[42] H. Mann, "How Real Are Friendships of Gifted and Typical Children in a Program of Partial Segregation?" *Exceptional Children* (1957), pp. 199–201.
[43] J. A. Kahl, "Educational and Occupational Aspirations of 'Common Man' Boys," *Harvard Educational Review*, Vol. 23 (1953), pp. 186–203.
[44] H. Hyman, "The Value System of Different Classes: A Social Psychological Contribution to the Analysis of Stratification," in R. Bendix and S. M. Lipset (eds.), *Class, Status and Power* (Glencoe, Illinois: Free Press, 1953), pp. 426–442.
[45] Kahl, *loc. cit.*

ager's attitudes toward academic excellence would be positively related to his own ability and to the educational level attained by his parents.

SUMMARY

Various considerations combine to underscore the importance of a study of high school students' attitudes toward gifted peers. Deserving attention is an awareness of the current quest for skilled manpower; the possible existence of widespread anti-intellectual feelings and their effects on teen-agers; and the presence of strong conformity influences in the adolescent world.

Opinions regarding anti-intellectualism in America are important not merely for their sheer abundance; they also suggest the specific nature of generalizations made about learning and the learned. Unfortunately, research on adolescents' beliefs rarely assesses the extent to which negative verbal stereotypes are ascribed to the gifted. The little evidence that does exist, however, indicates that such attitudes may be operative in the teen-age world. There are studies pointing to the secondary importance of academic pursuits for their own sake at school, as perceived by youth as well as adults. Teen-agers apparently prefer being known as athletes or "wheels" rather than as "eggheads" or brilliant students. Yet sociometric investigations show that those with better-than-average ability have somewhat of an advantage in their social standing among peers, though it is not known whether they rate well because of their academic powers or because of nonintellective traits. Students with IQs above 150, on the other hand, show signs of serious difficulty in their relationships with schoolmates.

Except for the fact that self-betterment seems more highly valued among the gifted than among the nongifted, there is little evidence to determine adolescents' feelings about diligence in school work. Athletic-mindedness, on the other hand, is clearly esteemed by youth, and this raises questions about the extent to which possession of such a popular attribute can nullify whatever stigmatic effects (if any) there are in being brilliant (or average) and studious (or nonstudious).

Basically, therefore, this inquiry compared adolescent attitudes toward two types of high school students, one reputedly "brilliant" and the other "average" in ability. It further sought to ascertain whether possible differences in reaction to such types of students are affected by these contrasting ability characteristics independently or through interaction with certain other personal attributes, such as effort at school and athletic-mindedness. Also investigated were the degrees to which teen-agers' intelligence and parental education correlate with their acceptance ratings of the academically brilliant.

The specific questions raised were as follows:

1. What kinds of attitudes do adolescents express toward the academically "brilliant" as against the "average" high school student?

2. Do teen-agers differentiate between academic brilliance and average ability regardless of whether those possessing these attributes are also studious (or nonstudious) and athletic-minded (or nonathletic-minded)?

3. What kinds of attitudes do adolescents express toward the studious as against the nonstudious in high school?

4. What kinds of attitudes do adolescents express toward athletic- as against nonathletic-minded high school students?

5. Are there differences between male and female high school students in their attitudes toward academic brilliance (versus average ability), studiousness (versus nonstudiousness), and athletic-mindedness (versus nonathletic-mindedness)?

6. Is a high school student's attitude toward academic brilliance influenced by his own scholastic ability and the extent of his parents' formal schooling?

3

Techniques for Assessing
Adolescent Attitudes

The present investigation dealt with verbal stereotypes ascribed by high school students to several fictitious characters. Each character was represented by a written description of his ability at school, the amount of effort he expends on schoolwork and the extent of his interest and participation in sports. Attitudes were stimulated solely by this triad of statements.

Since the respondents dealt with a verbal report about a hypothetical person rather than a live being, it is important at the outset to differentiate between the two types of experience. In a face-to-face meeting, each participant defines the "objective" characteristics of the other in his own way. The observer reacts to distinctive attributes which derive from a universe of perceptions he has *himself* assembled, and he makes his evaluation accordingly. One can never assume that those who agree or differ in their general opinions about anyone are all reacting to the same array of characteristics. Traits seen as crucial by one observer may be inconspicuous or even nonexistent in the eyes of another observer of the same person. This implies that there are probably as many individualities for any one person as there are observers of him. It is therefore possible that conflicting attitudes toward live humans are born not only out of contrasting value orientations but out of differences in cognition as well.

Less subjective are the identifying traits of an imaginary character. Here the portrait is structured *for* the observer rather than *by* him, and since the given information is uniform for all respondents, there can be no disagreement about its content. Reactions to a verbal report about someone are perforce controlled by the given material plus whatever information may be read into it. There is less mystery as to what, precisely, is triggering off reactions in this case than in the case of a live encounter between two people.

Another a priori factor to consider is the basic difference between representing an imaginary character in terms of personal attributes as against other classificatory labels. When people are asked to ascribe verbal stereotypes to a foreign or minority group, the responses are to a class of individuals whose membership is clearly defined. Observers may agree or disagree about the traits that typify Negroes, Germans, or Turks, but there is generally no quarrel regarding a given person's membership in one of these groups. Consequently, to the extent that verbal stereotypes associated with national and color groups are predictive of face-to-face reactions to individual representatives, one can learn something about the social status of persons to whom these attitudes apply.

In contrast to the fairly unanimous agreement on the identity of members of nationalities, it is more difficult to find such agreement about a live person's fitting the description of a hypothetical one where the information given deals with his academic ability, studiousness, and athletic-mindedness. One who is regarded as brilliant by some may be perceived as only average or somewhat above average by others. The same division of opinion is possible also with respect to his effort at school and his interest and participation in sports. This makes it that much more difficult to predict face-to-face reactions to any *actual* persons from a knowledge of the verbal stereotypes ascribed to imaginary characters.

Worthy of note, too, is the fact that the language used in depicting a character may strongly influence patterns of reactions to him. Describing one as "academically brilliant" and another as "academically average" may evoke one pattern of contrasting responses, while such descriptions as "academically bright" against "academically average" or "mental giant" against "fair student" or "a brain" against "a typical teen-ager," might result in different response patterns.

With these basic premises established, it will be easier to understand in what specific ways the main objectives of the present study were served by its design.

INSTRUMENTATION OF THE STUDY

Background for Designing the Instrument

The design of the instrument[1] was derived from two others administered in previous research on attitudes expressed through verbal stereotypes. One was developed by Katz and Braly[2] in their study of generalizations

[1] The form of the final questionnaire is give in Appendix B.
[2] D. Katz and K. W. Braly, "Verbal Stereotypes and Racial Prejudice," in T. M. Newcomb and E. L. Hartley (eds.), *Readings in Social Psychology* (New York: Henry Holt & Company, 1947).

made about racial and national groups, and the other by Goodman[3] in his study of impressions stimulated by verbal descriptions of hypothetical individuals. Katz and Braly asked twenty-five college students to list whatever traits they thought typical of each of ten racial and national groups. From this list, one hundred other students then selected what to them were the most appropriate traits describing each of the cultural classifications. Another student group then rated each of the selected adjectives on the basis of its desirability in friends and associates. The researchers could thus learn not only the distinctive verbal stereotypes associated with each of the ten racial and national groups but also the relative acceptability of these groups based on the frequency with which desirable and undesirable traits were associated with them. When a fourth committee of college students arranged the groups in rank order with respect to preference of association with their members, it was revealed that the preferential rankings and the relative standings on the basis of associated traits were similar.

In Goodman's study, a carefully designed mixture of four characteristics making up the descriptions of hypothetical characters enabled the investigator to see whether or not slight changes in the descriptions could provoke change in reactions to these characters. In one series of patterns, each of sixteen stimulus characters was described in four sentences, each sentence containing either the desirable or undesirable member of a pair of contrasting characteristics. The first sentence described the character either as "thrifty" or "wasteful"; the second, either as "patient" or "impatient"; the third, either as "prompt" or "not prompt"; and the final sentence, either as "obedient" or "disobedient." It was therefore possible to predict to some degree a preferential ranking that would generally be agreed upon for these stimulus characters by merely counting the number of positive and negative qualities that went into the makeup of each one.

Goodman found that junior high school students were sensitive enough to the subtle variations among combinations of attributes to be capable of ascribing to each character the traits appropriate for him in terms of his individuality and social distance rating in relation to the other fifteen.

In view of the research objectives attained by Katz and Braly and by Goodman, it was felt that adopting some features of the instruments used in their studies would be advantageous in the present investigation. Like the Katz and Braly instrument, the one used here was designed to reveal both the relative acceptance of several hypothetical characters and the specific traits contributing to each character's rating. As in the case of the

---

[3] S. M. Goodman, "Forming Impressions of Persons from Verbal Report" (Unpublished Doctoral Dissertation, Teachers College, Columbia University, 1950).

Goodman study, the instrument also called for reactions to combinations of attributes that vary systematically from one stimulus character to the next.

Construction of the Instrument

1. *Creating the stimulus characters.* The initial step in constructing the questionnaire was the development of a series of imaginary stimulus characters. Each character was described in three sentences. The first sentence referred to academic ability (brilliant or average); the second to effort in school work (studious or nonstudious); and the third to sports-mindedness (athletic or nonathletic). The three dichotomized personal qualities appeared in every possible combination, thus creating descriptions of eight stimulus characters.

The first sentence in each description, referring to *academic ability,* appeared either as

Brilliant: "Pupil X is a *brilliant* high school student who is always among the *highest* in class in all academic subjects."

or

Average: "Pupil X is an *average* student who receives *fair* grades in all academic subjects."

The second sentence in each description, referring to *effort,* appeared either as

Studious: "Pupil X spends *more* time at home studying school subjects and doing homework than do most students."

or

Nonstudious: "Pupil X spends *no more* time at home studying school subjects and doing homework than do most students."

The third sentence in each description, referring to *sports-mindedness,* appeared either as

Athletic: "Pupil X *is* sports-minded and participates in *many* athletic activities at school."

or

Nonathletic: "Pupil X *is not* sports-minded and *does not* participate in many athletic activities at school."

The eight stimulus characters resulted as follows:

1
BRILLIANT
STUDIOUS
ATHLETIC

Pupil A is a *brilliant* high school student who is always among the *highest* in class in all academic subjects. Pupil A spends *more* time studying school subjects and doing homework than do most students. Pupil A *is* sports-minded and participates in *many* athletic activities at school.

2
AVERAGE
NONSTUDIOUS
ATHLETIC

Pupil B is an *average* student who receives *fair* grades in all academic subjects. Pupil B spends *no more* time at home studying school subjects and doing homework than do most students. Pupil B *is* sports-minded and participates in *many* athletic activities at school.

3
BRILLIANT
NONSTUDIOUS
ATHLETIC

Pupil C is a *brilliant* high school student who is always among the *highest* in class in all academic subjects. Pupil C spends *no more* time at home studying school subjects and doing homework than do most sudents. Pupil C *is* sports-minded and participates in *many* athletic activities at school.

4
AVERAGE
STUDIOUS
ATHLETIC

Pupil D is an *average* student who receives *fair* grades in all academic subjects. Pupil D spends *more* time at home studying school subjects and doing homework than do most students. Pupil D *is* sports-minded and participates in *many* athletic activities at school.

5
BRILLIANT
NONSTUDIOUS
NONATHLETIC

Pupil E is a *brilliant* high school student who is always among the *highest* in class in all academic subjects. Pupil E spends *no more* time at home studying school subjects and doing homework than do most students. Pupil E *is not* sports-minded and *does not* participate in many athletic activities at school.

6
AVERAGE
NONSTUDIOUS
NONATHLETIC

Pupil F is an *average* student who receives *fair* grades in all academic subjects. Pupil F spends *no more* time at home studying school subjects and doing homework than do most students. Pupil F *is not* sports-minded and *does not* participate in many athletic activities at school.

7
BRILLIANT
STUDIOUS
NONATHLETIC

Pupil G is a *brilliant* high school student who is always among the *highest* in class in all academic subjects. Pupil G spends *more* time at home studying school subjects and doing homework than do most students. Pupil G *is not* sports-minded and *does not* participate in many athletic activities at school.

8
AVERAGE
STUDIOUS
NONATHLETIC

Pupil H is an *average* student who receives *fair* grades in all academic subjects. Pupil H spends *more* time at home studying school subjects and doing homework than do most students. Pupil H *is not* sports-minded and *does not* participate in many athletic activities at school.

Since the descriptions were composed of statements rather than listings of characteristics, attention should be drawn to what this may imply in terms of the study's design. The first and third sentences identify the stimulus characters not merely by the labels "brilliant" (or "average") and "sports-minded" (or "not sports-minded"), but a brief explanation further defining the meaning of these labels is presented. In the second sentence the information is given not through labels but through a comparison of the character's industriousness at school work to a familiar, though vague, norm. As a result, the descriptions left less to the selective perceptions of the respondents and provided stimuli which could evoke more or less common perceptions. The traits attributed to the characters would, therefore, be more apt to reflect varied attitudes toward commonly perceived individuals. The descriptions also provided more clear-cut criteria for judging whether or not they can apply to live individuals, although there remained much room for disagreement on that score.

The sex of the character was not mentioned in any description, in order to determine how suggestive of gender are the stimulus characteristics themselves. To secure this information, the respondents were asked to indicate whether each character was a "boy," a "girl," or "either one."

2. *Building the trait list.* The second step was to develop a list of traits each of which would be judged as descriptive (or not) of every stimulus character. In order to accomplish this, a simple questionnaire was sent to some 200 students in several urban, suburban, and rural high schools, asking them to list separately those adjectives and descriptive phrases they thought typical of the brilliant student and of the outstanding athlete. The lists were then combined and arranged, wherever possible, in trait clusters, each containing a group of synonyms and antonyms. This made possible the selection of a single trait or two from every cluster to represent the thought expressed by that group of descriptive terms. For example, the traits "shy" and "quiet" were chosen to represent the following group suggested by the 200 teen-agers canvassed:[4]

Doesn't have much to say	Shy
Hides his feelings	Quiet
Introvert	Talker
Mostly listening instead of talking	Talkative
Not too talkative	Very forward

Added to these representative traits were those that did not fit in clusters, despite the fact that some were mentioned by no more than one of the respondents. The number of traits was thus pared down to 54, and they were listed beneath every character with instructions to circle a "yes" or "no" next to each trait, depending on whether or not it was thought to be typical of the particular character.

[4] See Appendix A for further examples of trait clusters.

An effort was made to preserve the language in which the traits were originally couched, and colloquial terms such as "creep" and "brain" were also included. The only change in original terminology was in the case of adjectives with negative modifiers, such as "not sociable." The trait was presented instead as "sociable" to avoid confronting the respondent with the possible task or having to express a positive attitude through double negatives. The negatives were retained, however, in three descriptive phrases (e.g., "Can't get a date"; "Doesn't have much fun"; and "Doesn't care for the opposite sex") because converting these to positive expressions would have partly destroyed the flavor of the original terminology.

3. *Rating the traits.* The final step involved asking a group of 106 students in a single suburban high school to rate each of the 54 traits as either desirable or undesirable. For a trait to be classified as either desirable or undesirable at least 70 per cent of the group had to agree on its nature. When there was less than 70 per cent agreement the trait was listed in the neutral category.

On the basis of the ratings by the 106 students, 27 traits were classified as desirable and 19 as undesirable. Eight traits were classified as neutral. Table 1 indicates the percentages of judges designating each trait as "desirable" and "undesirable."

Some of the traits apparently had dual implications which prevented clear-cut agreement as to their desirability. "Quiet," for example, might have been interpreted either as the absence of loud-mouth tendencies and thus desirable, or as dull and uncommunicative and thus undesirable. "Wears glasses" may have appeared as desirable to those who saw it as correcting defective vision, while others may have associated it with the sickly, unathletic youngsters whose faulty vision results from too much contact with books. Some might have interpreted "thin" as lack of good health, while others might have thought in terms of control of calorie intake. "Sticks with his or (her) own crowd" might have meant loyalty to the group, a desirable trait, or attachment to a clique, an undesirable trait. To be "studious" and "partake in many extracurricular activities" may have been viewed as excessive preoccupation with school work or as good school citizenship, and "serious" could have been seen as freedom from flightiness or as brooding dullness. Finally, a "brain" might have been seen by some as excessively absorbed in striving for academic success, while others might have seen it as a mark of accomplishment to be admired and appreciated.

TABLE 1:   PERCENTAGE OF HIGH SCHOOL STUDENTS DESIGNATING EACH
TRAIT AS "DESIRABLE" AND "UNDESIRABLE" (N=106)

Trait	Percentage Voting Desirable	Percentage Voting Undesirable	Percentage Not Voting
1. Good sport[a]	97.2	2.8	—
2. Perfectionist[b]	27.4	70.8	1.9
3. Teacher's pet[b]	3.8	96.2	—
4. Brain[c]	33	67	—
5. Walking dictionary[b]	9.4	90.6	—
6. Good school citizen[a]	92.5	7.6	—
7. Bookworm[b]	5.7	94.3	—
8. Creep[b]	1	99	—
9. Good conversationalist[a]	92.5	6.6	1
10. Good leader[a]	92.5	7.6	—
11. Spoiled[b]	2.8	97.2	—
12. Serious[c]	64.2	32.1	3.8
13. Nervous[b]	3.8	96.2	—
14. Competitive[a]	80.2	17.9	1.9
15. Proud of his (her) school work[a]	81.1	17.9	1
16. Conscientious[a]	79.3	19.8	1
17. Dull[b]	1	99	—
18. Mature[a]	95.3	4.8	—
19. Cheerful[a]	100	—	—
20. Shy[b]	8.5	89.6	1.9
21. Kind[a]	95.3	2.8	1.9
22. Nice looking[a]	91.5	8.5	—
23. Obedient[a]	78.3	19.8	1.9
24. Thin[c]	27.4	68.9	3.8
25. Stuck-up[b]	2.8	97.2	—
26. Studious[c]	60.4	37.7	1.9
27. Quiet[c]	35.9	61.3	2.8
28. Popular[a]	82.1	16	1.9
29. Sociable[a]	94.3	5.7	—
30. Healthy[a]	98.1	1.9	—
31. Bright[a]	91.5	7.6	1
32. Has good manners[a]	97.2	2.8	—
33. Has a pleasing personality[a]	99.1	1	—
34. Has good study habits[a]	84.9	14.2	1
35. Has an open mind to all situations[a]	92.5	7.6	—
36. Has good ideas[a]	98.1	1	1
37. Has an answer for every question[b]	17	83	—

TABLE 1, *Continued*

Trait	Percentage Voting Desirable	Percentage Voting Undesirable	Percentage Not Voting
38. Has a well-rounded life[a]	95.3	4.8	—
39. Takes criticism well[a]	87.7	10.4	1.9
40. Brags about his (her) marks[b]	3.8	96.2	—
41. Complains about never knowing enough[b]	14.2	85.9	—
42. Dislikes kids who get high marks[b]	13.2	86.8	—
43. Likes school[a]	69.8	29.3	1
44. Talks about you behind your back[b]	4.7	95.3	—
45. Sticks with his (her) own crowd[c]	32.1	63.2	4.7
46. Dresses well[a]	95.3	4.7	—
47. Wears glasses[c]	42.5	43.4	14.2
48. Expresses himself (herself) well[a]	96.2	3.8	—
49. In many extracurricular activities[c]	66	32.1	1.9
50. Can take responsibility[a]	97.2	2.9	—
51. Believes in all school work and no play[b]	—	100	—
52. Can't get a date[b]	12.3	86.8	1
53. Doesn't have much fun[b]	3.8	96.2	—
54. Doesn't care for the opposite sex[b]	8.5	91.6	—

[a] Denotes a desirable trait by virtue of 70 per cent or more students agreeing it is so.

[b] Denotes an undesirable trait by virtue of 70 per cent or more students agreeing it is so.

[c] Denotes a neutral trait by virtue of less than 70 per cent agreement on its being desirable or undesirable.

Scoring Procedures

When judgments of the traits were obtained, it was then possible to develop numerical ratings for each stimulus character as indicative of the attitudes toward him. When a respondent circled the "yes" for a desirable trait to signify that it typified a given character, the response was scored +1. A similar response for an undesirable trait was scored —1. Conversely, "no" responses for desirable traits were scored —1, and for undesirable traits, +1. Zero scores were assigned to the omissions as well as to "yes" and "no" responses to neutral traits. Thus, three possible kinds of scores for a stimulus character could be computed: (1) a global score representing the sum of positive evaluations ("yes" responses for desirable traits and "no" responses for undesirable traits) minus the sum of negative evaluations ("no" responses for desirable traits and "yes" responses for undesirable traits); (2) a desirable trait score (obtained by subtracting the number of "no" from the "yes" responses for all the desirable traits); and (3) an undesirable trait score (obtained by subtracting the number of "yes" from the "no" responses for the undesirable traits). For each of these ratings, the higher the score, the more positive the evaluation.

Since the respondents were forced to choose between "yes" and "no" on every trait, it was possible to derive a preferential rating of the eight characters not only on the basis of the entire trait list but also with respect to any single trait. The individuality of characters could thus be compared in terms of the traits distinctively associated or unassociated with each. For example, the trait "conscientious" was regarded as typifying one of the eight characters above all others by virtue of the fact that the trait score (total "yes" votes minus total "no" votes for "conscientious") was highest for that particular character. However, the forced choice also imposed some judgment difficulty on the respondents. Although Goodman's study demonstrated that readers of an imaginary character tend to ascribe to him traits that are not contained in his description, the respondents in the present study were compelled to expand their assignment of traits even further. In many instances they may have felt there was nothing in the information given about a stimulus character that suggested whether or not a certain trait on the list typified him. For example, all were forced to indicate whether the trait "shy" typified each character even though some may have been convinced there was nothing in the character descriptions to offer a clue one way or the other. Nevertheless, they had to make the decision in every case. Under such circumstances there was danger of internal inconsistency among the responses to individual characters, thus necessitating a careful check on the reliability of the instrument. (For reliability coefficients, see Table 2.)

Plan for Administering the Instrument

The description of each of the eight stimulus characters, followed by a list of 54 traits, was placed on a separate page. These pages, along with a questionnaire seeking background information about the respondent, were stapled together and distributed to each of the subjects in the study. (See Appendix B.)

In order to examine whether or not the position of each stimulus character in the sequence influenced responses, the order of the paragraphs was changed from one test booklet to the next so that each of the eight characters appeared in each of the eight positions. An analysis was then made to determine whether the ordinal position of any stimulus character affected his rating significantly. The result showed that it made no difference whether the respondents reacted to a given character before or after they had reacted to any of the others, insofar as his global score was concerned. In other words, it was not necessary to exercise care about the order in which the characters appeared in the booklet, for the results would have been the same regardless of the order.[5]

Although the plan for administering the instrument provided for the rotation of the position of the sequences, there was no similar provision for the rotation of the three basic elements in the descriptions. The first sentence always referred to ability, the second to effort, and the third to athleticism. Responses might have been different if these elements were arranged in other sequences, especially in view of Asch's[6] findings that reactions to imaginary persons described by a list of traits are influenced not only by the nature of the traits, but by their sequence. There is nothing in his study, however, to indicate whether the sequence of a series of descriptive sentences is as influential on reactions as the sequence of a list of traits. For practical purposes the present instrument did not rotate the descriptive sentences since such rotation would have resulted in 48 instead of 8 different paragraphs—a far too cumbersome instrument either for administration or scoring.

Reliability of the Instrument

Since a forced-choice type of response was called for, there was the danger of respondents having to make judgments without enough clues from the descriptions. Some respondents did, in fact, complain about this. Others criticized the instrument because they had to make generalizations hastily and to think in terms of stereotypes, habits often discouraged by their teachers. Nevertheless, the internal consistency of their responses revealed that they apparently conjured up clear pictures of the hypothetical characters and that they had fairly well-defined attitudes toward each of them. As indicated in Table 2, split-half reliability coefficients, obtained separately for scores on desirable and undesirable traits, and based on 65 completed questionnaires selected randomly for each character, reached .8 or higher for every stimulus character after corrections were made with the Spearman-Brown formula.

Intercorrelations among Character Scores

Table 7 in Appendix C shows an intercorrelational matrix of scores for desirable and undesirable traits, all of which were computed, in this case, by subtracting the numbers of "no" from "yes" responses. As the table

---

[5] For a two-way analysis of variance (stimulus characters vs. orders) see Appendix C, Table 1.

[6] S. E. Asch, "Forming Impressions of Personality," *Journal of Abnormal and Social Psychology,* Vol. 41 (1946), pp. 258–290.

TABLE 2: SPLIT-HALF RELIABILITY COEFFICIENTS[a] ON SCORES[b] FOR
DESIRABLE AND UNDESIRABLE TRAITS ASCRIBED TO EIGHT STIMULUS
CHARACTERS *(10 per cent Random Sample of Total Population
for Each Stimulus Character)*

Stimulus Characters	Desirable Traits	Undesirable Traits
Brilliant-Nonstudious-Athletic	.86	.82
Average-Nonstudious-Athletic	.92	.85
Average-Studious-Athletic	.90	.88
Brilliant-Studious-Athletic	.94	.87
Brilliant-Nonstudious-Nonathletic	.88	.92
Average-Nonstudious-Nonathletic	.89	.91
Average-Studious-Nonathletic	.89	.88
Brilliant-Studious-Nonathletic	.91	.80

[a] Spearman-Brown correction formula used in all computations.
[b] Computed as follows: sum of "yes" votes minus sum of "no" votes.

indicates, the correlation coefficient between scores on the two kinds of traits for each character was negative. This was to be expected, since there would logically tend to be an inverse relationship between the numbers of desirable and undesirable traits ascribed to the various characters. However, the highest inverse correlation reached only —.55, which suggests that the two groups of traits were not measuring precise opposites of the same dimensions of social status. Moreover, what may be indicated here is that the negativism expressed by denying someone's possession of desirable traits is quite different from that shown by attaching undesirable traits to him. Similarly, ascribing desirable traits to an individual might have indicated a level of acceptability different from that implied by denying the presence of undesirable traits.

POPULATION TESTED

The population on which the basic survey was taken came from a single New York City comprehensive high school located in a thickly settled residential area of Brooklyn. Attending classes were some 3,700 boys and girls, approximately three fourths Jewish, 20 per cent Negroes and Puerto Ricans, and the rest from a small number of Italian families. The school draws its students from a predominantly middle-income community, populated mostly by shopkeepers, professionals, salesmen, and white-collar workers. Some 30 per cent of the respondents' parents owned small businesses, another 16 per cent were professionals, and the rest worked at various kinds of jobs in offices, factories, and stores. Many were immigrants whose formal education had been curtailed when they left their country of origin or soon afterward.

For some students, education at this school is terminal; others go on to college or other places of higher learning. Of those who enter, 79 per cent are graduated with one of three kinds of certificates: an academic diploma, granted to 67 per cent of the graduates; a commercial diploma, conferred on 11 per cent of the graduates; and a general diploma, given to 22 per cent of the graduates. School officials claim that nearly three fourths of those earning academic diplomas plan on posthigh school education of some kind.

The instrument was administered to 615 eleventh graders drawn from a large representative sample of honor, regular, and modified English classes. Since English is one of the core of subjects that all students are required to take, regardless of which diploma they pursue, it was felt that the best representation of the junior year would be found in these classes. A full 45-minute period was allotted to each testing session and most respondents found that it was ample time to complete the questionnaire.

BACKGROUND INFORMATION ON STUDENTS AND THEIR PARENTS

Parents' Education

Levels of schooling were scaled from one to six, as follows:
1. Attended elementary school
2. Graduated from elementary school
3. Attended high school
4. Graduated from high school
5. Attended college
6. Graduated from college

Respondents were asked to check the item descriptive of the highest level of schooling reached by each parent, and the appropriate scale ratings were recorded accordingly.

Scholastic Ability

Because of time limitation, it was agreed that a test of scholastic ability would have to be brief so that it could be administered along with the rest of the instrument in one school period. Selected was the Thorndike 20-word vocabulary measure, a sharply graded test which includes two words from each of the ten levels of the vocabulary section of the I.E.R. Intelligence Scale of C.A.V.D.[7] It was standardized on a voting sample of the American Institute of Public Opinion and proved to be a dependable measure of ability.

DATA ANALYSIS PROCEDURES

Statistical Approach

The basic statistical model for examining the results was a three-way analysis of variance of mean global scores ascribed to the eight characters. This was done for the total population and separately for the male and female subgroups. As indicated in Figure 1, such a block design is particularly suited to a study involving three dichotomous variables where every possible factor (ability, effort, and athleticism in this case) can be analyzed independently and in its interaction with the other factors. Through this design, for example, such questions as "Does the character's ability, or effort, or athletic-mindedness *separately* make a difference in his global rating?"; or "Does the character's ability in combination with the kind of effort and/or sports interests he shows make a difference in his global score?" can be answered. By employing the Scheffé[8] test comparisons could be made of reactions to the eight characters individually or in subcombinations.

The Scheffé method tests individual mean differences and also makes possible the comparison of one group of means against another or against a single mean. In every application, the formula provides a method of determining how large the gap must be between individual or group means in order to reach significance at a selected level. Thus, comparisons could be made of the brilliant characters as a group with those of average ability matched for effort and athleticism. Kerlinger referred to the Scheffé test as "rather conservative . . . if we get a significant difference with this test, we can be quite sure that it is really significant, whereas a *t* test might show spurious significance."[9]

Qualitative Analysis

In order to ascertain which traits were most consistently descriptive of the various characters, the total "no" responses were subtracted from the

---

[7] R. L. Thorndike, "Two Screening Tests of Verbal Intelligence," *Journal of Applied Psychology,* Vol. 26 (1942), pp. 128–135. The instrument was used with permission of the Institute of Psychological Research, Teachers College, Columbia University.

[8] H. Scheffé, "A Method for Judging All Contrasts in the Analysis of Variance," *Biometrika,* Vol. 40 (1953), pp. 87–104.

[9] F. H. Kerlinger, *Research Design and Analysis of Variance* (New York: New York University, School of Education, 1957), p. 16.

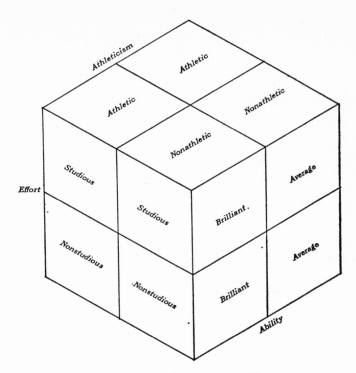

FIGURE 1.   BLOCK DESIGN FOR A THREE-WAY
ANALYSIS OF VARIANCE

total "yes" responses for each trait separately for every character. Resulting from this procedure were eight different scores per trait, one for each
of the characters. These eight scores were then ranked from highest to
lowest (1 to 8), thus indicating which characters were most (and least)
typified by the given trait. The traits associated and unassociated with the
characters actually made each one a distinctive being, recognizable in
terms of personal qualities attached to him.

Background Factors

Determining the degrees of association between background factors and
attitudes toward the stimulus characters involved testing for linear relationships. Correlation coefficients were therefore computed separately
for relationships of ratings on father's education, mother's education, and
vocabulary score, with global scores ascribed to each character. These
coefficients were then examined for significance and for information on
how much of the variance they explain.

4

Adolescent Reactions to
Academic Brilliance

The objectives of this study were pursued by (1) studying the ratings of the eight stimulus characters; (2) comparing the reactions to individual and combinations of characteristics; (3) locating the traits distinctively associated and unassociated with each character; (4) measuring the degree of association between background factors and the ratings of the characters; and (5) comparing male and female respondents' reactions to the characters and characteristics.

A quick impression of human attributes admired and derogated by adolescents may be gained by noting which of the 54 traits they considered desirable and which they regarded as undesirable (see Table 1, pp. 27–28). The group of teen-agers judging the traits reacted positively to those revealing a love of fun, the ability to socialize harmoniously with peers, moderate success at school, good physical health, and personal attractiveness. They tended to belittle the traits denoting excessive devotion to school work, inability to achieve good social rapport with one's own and opposite sex, and the possession of certain deviant personal habits. There is a suggestion also of allegiance to the golden mean in some of these ratings. Although being "bright" and "conscientious" drew positive reactions, the students were not as accepting of such traits as "brain," "a walking dictionary," and "believes in all school work and no play." The teen-agers also thought well of one who is "proud of his (her) school work" but were critical of one who "brags about his (her) marks" or "complains about never knowing enough." These ratings provided an early hint of what personal qualities lead to social acceptability and rejection in the adolescent world.

HOW THE STIMULUS CHARACTERS WERE RATED

Figure 2 shows the mean global scores for each of the eight stimulus characters, ranked from highest to lowest. Rated at the top was the bril-

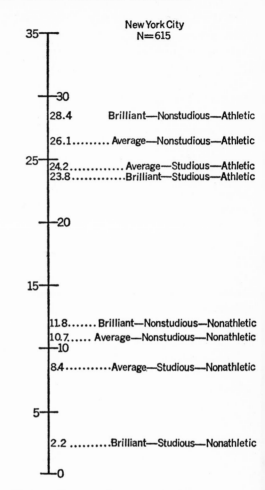

FIGURE 2.   MEAN GLOBAL SCORES ASCRIBED TO THE
EIGHT STIMULUS CHARACTERS

liant–nonstudious athlete, followed closely by the three other athletes. The two successively ranked characters showing the largest difference in mean global scores were the lowest rated among the athletes (the brilliant–studious–athletic) and the highest rated among the nonathletes (the brilliant–nonstudious–nonathletic). The only other character scoring significantly lower than the one preceding him in rank was the brilliant-studious–nonathletic, ranked eighth and therefore the lone isolate in the group. Rated first and second among athletes and nonathletes were those described also as nonstudious. As for the brilliant characters, they ranked first and last among the athletes and nonathletes. All stimulus characters received positive mean global scores.

A comparison of mean global scores (Appendix C, Table 3) shows no significant difference in the ratings of the two nonstudious athletes (brilliant and average), who ranked first and second. However, the brilliant–nonstudious athlete rated significantly higher than the two studious athletes as well as all the nonathletes. The second ranked average–nonstudious athlete, on the other hand, did not differ significantly from any of the other athletes. For the nonathletic characters, there were no significant differences among the three ranked highest, although each of these characters rated significantly better than the last-place brilliant–studious nonathlete.

The character ratings make it clear that brilliance in and of itself was regarded as fully acceptable as average ability. What determined the estimate of a character was not the nature of his ability as such, but rather the nature of *other* stimulus characteristics *in combination* with his ability. Being brilliant or average made little difference, insofar as the character's global score was concerned, provided he was also nonstudious and athletic-minded. Nor did brilliance matter either way for those described also as studious athletes or as nonstudious nonathletes. But where the stimulus character was studious and indifferent to sports he was penalized considerably more for being also brilliant as opposed to average in ability.

The global scores for the stimulus characters also point up the incredibly high regard attached to athletic-mindedness. Not only was every athlete rated much higher than any of the nonathletes, but within the group of four athletic characters the difference from highest to lowest score was less than 5 points, which, though significant, is small considering that the highest score for all eight characters exceeded the lowest by more than 26 points. This shows that an interest and participation in sports had a strong, though not complete, stabilizing effect on the estimates of the characters regardless of their ability and effort at school. Toward the nonathletic characters, however, there was greater differentiation of attitudes as evidenced by the fact that the highest global score exceeded the lowest by more than 9 points. In this group the brilliant–studious character stands in disfavor relative to all the other nonathletes, which is not true for his counterpart among the athletes. Apparently, the disadvantage of being nonathletic is not as uniformly strong for all as the advantage of being an athlete.

RATINGS OF CHARACTERISTICS SINGLY AND IN COMBINATION

Analyses[1] were made of the differential reactions to *ability* (brilliance vs. averageness); *effort* (studiousness vs. nonstudiousness); and *athleticism* (athletic vs. nonathletic). Results show that the respondents expressed no preferences in the choice between brilliance and average ability. With respect to *effort* and *athleticism,* however, the ratings definitely favored nonstudiousness and athletic-mindedness.

In the ratings of combinations of characteristics some important reactions were noted.[2] These became evident through a comparison of the combined mean global scores of pairs of stimulus characters identical in two characteristics though different in the third. For example, in one such analysis a mean rating was obtained for four pairs of characters, each pair consisting of those with the same *ability* and *effort* characteristics, but opposite in terms of *athleticism.* This facilitated a four-way comparison of the two brilliant–studious vs. the two brilliant–nonstudious vs. the two average–studious vs. the two average–nonstudious characters. Every pair included one athlete and one nonathlete (see Figure 3), thus nullifying the effects of athleticism on the ratings of *ability* and *effort* in combination. Of these four pairs, the most highly rated were the brilliant–nonstudious characters, followed by those described as average–nonstudious, average–studious, and brilliant–studious, in that order. There were no significant differences between the pairs of characters ranked first and second, nor between those ranked second and third. But the brilliant–studious characters, rated fourth and therefore lowest, were significantly less acceptable than the average–studious characters, ranked immediately above them. From these ratings one can see clearly that there was no disadvantage to being brilliant as against average when these characteristics were combined with non-studiousness. However, brilliance was significantly *less* acceptable than average ability in characters described also as studious. Then too, it was considered far more desirable for the brilliant to be nonstudious than studious, whereas for those with average ability it did not matter either way.

A comparison was then made among four other pairs of characters, each pair consisting of those identical in *ability* and *athleticism,* but different in terms of *effort* (see Figure 4). Ranked first were the brilliant athletes, followed closely by the average ability athletes, and then, by considerable margins, the average and brilliant nonathletes, in that order.

[1] See Appendix C, Table 4, for three-way analysis of variance.
[2] See Appendix C, Table 4, for the interaction effects of *ability* and *effort; ability* and *athleticism;* and *effort* and *athleticism* in the three-way analysis of variance.

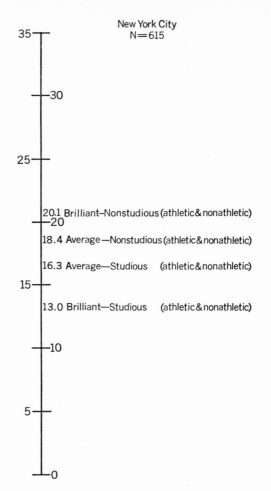

FIGURE 3.   MEAN GLOBAL SCORES ASCRIBED TO PAIRS OF
STIMULUS CHARACTERS IDENTICAL IN *Ability* AND *Effort*
BUT OPPOSITE IN *Athleticism*

The striking difference in the ratings of athletes as against nonathletes, regardless of their ability, demonstrates the persuasive role of sports-mindedness in the reactions to these characters. Yet of equal importance is the fact that there was no preference shown between brilliant and average athletes, while the average nonathletes were rated significantly higher than the brilliant nonathletes. In other words, the attitude expressed was that it doesn't matter whether the student is brilliant or average so long

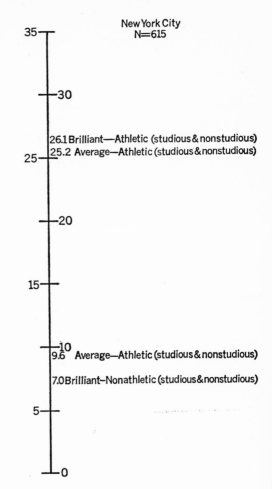

New York City
N=615

35

30

26.1 Brilliant—Athletic (studious & nonstudious)
25.2 Average—Athletic (studious & nonstudious)

25

20

15

10
9.6 Average—Athletic (studious & nonstudious)

7.0 Brilliant–Nonathletic (studious & nonstudious)

5

0

FIGURE 4.   MEAN GLOBAL SCORES ASCRIBED TO PAIRS OF
CHARACTERS IDENTICAL IN *Ability* AND *Athleticism* BUT
OPPOSITE IN *Effort*

as he is also athletic-minded. However, if he is not athletic-minded it is
less acceptable for him to be also brilliant rather than average at school.

Finally, a comparison was made of combinations of characters having
the same *effort* and *athleticism* characteristics, but unlike in *ability* (see
Figure 5). Here the ratings differed significantly in every case, with the
nonstudious athletes at the top, far above the next-ranked studious ath-

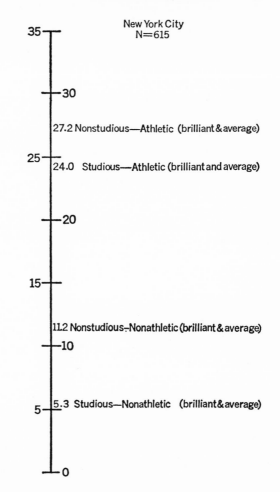

New York City
N=615

35

30

27.2 Nonstudious—Athletic (brilliant & average)

25

24.0 Studious—Athletic (brilliant and average)

20

15

11.2 Nonstudious—Nonathletic (brilliant & average)

10

5.3 Studious—Nonathletic (brilliant & average)

5

0

FIGURE 5.   MEAN GLOBAL SCORES ASCRIBED TO PAIRS OF
STIMULUS CHARACTERS IDENTICAL IN *Effort* AND
Athleticism BUT DIFFERENT IN *Ability*

letes who, in turn, scored considerably higher than the nonstudious nonathletes and the studious nonathletes, the latter pair rating lowest by a
wide margin. Expressed in these scores was the feeling that nonstudiousness is definitely preferable to its counterpart regardless of whether the
character is athletic or nonathletic. Likewise, the desirability of interest in
sports holds true for the studious as well as the nonstudious. Nevertheless,

it is interesting to note that the respondents discriminated to a greater extent between the studious and nonstudious when these characters were nonathletes than when they were athletes. Moreover, the choice of athletes over nonathletes was sharper among the studious than among the nonstudious characters. This shows that although *effort* and *athleticism* swayed student reaction independently they had their combined effects as well.

EVIDENCE FROM OTHER SCHOOLS

In order to determine the extent to which some of the results of this investigation could be generalized, efforts were made to replicate the study in several high schools outside New York City. Included were small samples from several rural communities in New York State and from Denver, Colorado. Although the results obtained were not analyzed statistically, the ranking of stimulus characters and characteristics resembled that obtained in the New York City school. No definitive conclusions can be drawn from such small samples, but enough evidence was assembled to suggest that the results in New York City are not peculiar to one high school in that community.

Somewhat different attitudes were expressed, however, by students in an upper middle-class city in Connecticut some thirty miles from New York City.[3] Three separate populations were surveyed there: a large group of eleventh graders, totaling 385, in a public high school; and much smaller samples from two private preparatory schools, one all-boys and the other all-girls.

Basically, the public high school population agreed with the adolescents in New York City and elsewhere (see Figure 6). As in the latter groups, brilliance and average ability were rated about equal, and athletic-mindedness was a decidedly desirable attribute. However, there seemed to be less stigma attached to studiousness in this school as indicated by the fact that, taken together, the studious rated about as well as the nonstudious characters. Here, too, it appeared that the combination of brilliance and athletic-mindedness was a highly fortunate one, whereas the combination of brilliance and lack of interest in sports was most undesirable.

In private preparatory schools (see Figures 7 and 8), the brilliant–studious–nonathletic character actually rose above last place in the ratings. There was a tendency to regard brilliance as slightly preferable to average ability, especially in the boys' school. Although these samples are too

[3] Appreciation is hereby expressed to Eva M. Taylor, a graduate student at Teachers College, Columbia University, for administering the questionnaire, scoring responses, and tabulating results.

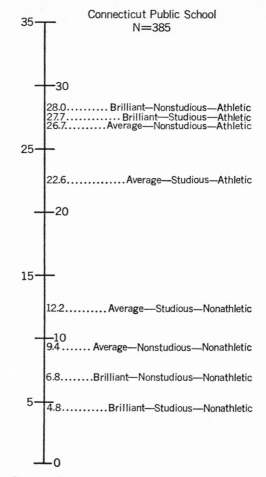

FIGURE 6.   Mean Global Scores Ascribed to the
Eight Stimulus Characters

small to be conclusively revealing, they do suggest that the atmosphere in some schools may not be embarrassing for one who demonstrates a keen mind and unusual devotion to studies.

Interpretation of Attitudes

The character ratings provide some telling insights into the status of academic brilliance in the adolescent world. If anything, they suggest the need to re-examine many pronouncements about negative attitudes toward

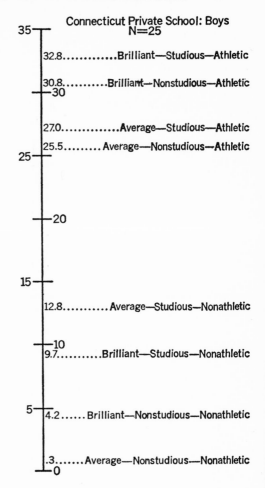

FIGURE 7.   MEAN GLOBAL SCORES ASCRIBED TO THE
EIGHT STIMULUS CHARACTERS

intellectualism allegedly pervading the nation's classrooms. The teen-
agers surveyed in the present study felt that brilliance (as against average
ability) had no particular attracting or repelling power. They seemed to
be saying that if the academically superior are victimized by prejudice
among peers, it is not due simply to the fact of being superior. Instead, it
results from the interaction of brilliance with other characteristics that are
relatively objectionable to adolescents. Only as part of an unfortunate
combination of qualities does brilliance serve as a leavening agent to produce a total unsavory impression.

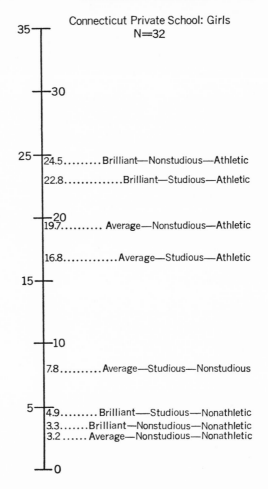

FIGURE 8.   MEAN GLOBAL SCORES ASCRIBED TO THE
EIGHT STIMULUS CHARACTERS

These findings also show that moderation with respect to scholastic effort was viewed favorably. In most of the schools surveyed, nonstudiousness was rated significantly higher than studiousness, which leads one to qualify Mead's thoughts regarding the valuation of diligence at school in this country. It may be true that teachers place greatest value on high academic status attained through hard work; however, the present findings suggest that adolescents do not share these attitudes. On the contrary, a more-than-average amount of time spent on study can lead to social penalties in the teen-age world, especially for the most able students.

Finally, the results underscore teen-agers' near-addiction to sports, thus confirming previous findings in the field. The incredible consistency with which athletes were rated preferable to nonathletes[4] demonstrates the socially redeeming powers of being sports-minded even if one possesses other characteristics that are not too acceptable among teen-agers. Neither the *ability* nor *effort* characteristics had nearly as decisive an effect on the character ratings as did *athleticism*.

Reactions to Academic Ability

Of particular significance were the reactions to characters reputed to be academically brilliant. The ratings show that brilliance at school can be respected or disparaged, depending on the personal attributes with which it mingles. Earning exceptionally high grades is as highly admired as average performance for the kind of youth who is known to spend no more time on school work than do most students and who is an interested participant in sports. However, the brilliant youth faces far more serious social penalties than his average-ability schoolmate if both show an uncommonly strong preoccupation with study and a lack of interest in sports. The academically outstanding high school student, it seems, can ill afford to earn the reputation of being studious and nonathletic. Conversely, the studious nonathlete must guard against rising too far above fair scholastic status lest he risk drawing ridicule from peers.

In essence, then, academic brilliance attracts negative verbal stereotypes when it is part of a nexus of characteristics perceived unfavorably by high school students. This is especially evidenced by reactions to the brilliant–studious nonathlete. Why was this character singled out as considerably less popular than the rest? Possibly because the teen-agers recognized a kind of logic and harmony in his constellation of attributes that facilitated disapproving judgments. Underlying their sentiments about him may have been the conviction that he has foolishly sacrificed powerful status-raising behaviors in order to succeed eminently at school. Or, perhaps earning high grades at the cost of so much effort and self-abnegation is not thought to be much of a feat. Haven't generations of schoolmarms and middle-class parents preached to children that anyone can reach academic excellence if he tries hard enough? The point is to accomplish it without excessive sweat and social isolation, without the special boosters, so to speak, that are often thought capable of propelling even ordinary minds to respectable heights.

The average student whose diligence at school is immoderate and who is not athletic-minded rates higher than his brilliant counterpart possibly

[4] As evidenced by an F ratio of more than 1,300. See Appendix C, Table 4.

because he is perceived as assuming a kind of spartan existence in order to avoid scholastic failure. It seems relatively acceptable to study hard and deny oneself certain pleasurable experiences in order to "keep one's head above water," academically. If so, it would appear that according to adolescents the golden mean in school achievement is a goal more worthy of striving toward than is outstanding success in one's studies. Moderate success in this instance has the advantage of preserving anonymity. A student earning average grades at school is not enough in the public eye to attract caustic reactions to his bookishness and certain verbal stereotypes reserved for the one who is "top dog" in his studies and viewed as self-sacrificing in his efforts to maintain that position.

Another kind of image that may have been conjured up by the description of the brilliant–studious nonathlete is that of a familiar caricature of the frail intellectual who would choose (or perhaps retreat to) a life of the mind in loneliness rather than engage in the more earthy experience prized by adolescents. He reminds one of the geniuses studied by Hollingworth,[5] whose difficulty in relating socially with age-mates may have been both a cause and effect of rejection by them. His brilliance is seen as a freakish quality, obscure in origin and perhaps worth coveting, but a definite handicap to his making friends if he compounds this deviance with atypical habits and values. He is the well-known "square," way out of touch with the crowd which feels threatened by his extraordinary mental powers should the accompanying social behavior also be nonconforming. There is no similar mystery or alien quality about averageness; most anyone can comprehend the work of an undistinguished mind. This "intellectual earthiness" may help induct the average student more comfortably into his peer group even if his behavior in other ways be regarded as uncommon.

An interesting question arising from these results is whether or not teen-agers' attitudes toward academic brilliance harmonize with those of their teachers and parents. Specifically, do these feelings constitute another bit of old-fashioned adolescent rebelliousness, or are adults inclined to share (and even inspire) them in private though they may inveigh against them in public? Although no definitive answers are yet available, two surveys offer some provocative clues. In one survey by the author, some one hundred graduate students in two education courses were asked to rank the eight stimulus characters in terms of the kinds of sons and daughters they would like to have and in terms of the kinds of people they would prefer to teach. The results showed that these professional

[5] Leta S. Hollingworth, *Children Above 180 IQ: Origin and Development* (Yonkers, New York: World Book Company, 1942).

educators were more favorably disposed toward academic brilliance than were the high school students. Although they tended to favor nonstudiousness and athletic-mindedness, as did the teen-agers in this study, they also ranked the brilliant characters as a group appreciably higher than the average-ability characters.

In another survey conducted by Coleman[6] parents were found to be more strongly attracted to the ideal of the "brilliant" student than were their teen-age sons and daughters. They expressed a wish for their children to become outstanding scholars far more often than their children expressed it for themselves. Yet these teen-agers thought their parents would be prouder of their child's success in making the basketball team (in the case of boys) or in becoming a cheer leader (in the case of girls) than in being chosen to serve as a biology assistant. This conflicting perception of parental attitudes suggests that if parents admire academic pursuits as strongly as they claim, such feelings have not been adequately communicated to their children. Perhaps they are willing to suppress their own opinions in favor of supporting their teen-agers' quest for status among peers. What the adult may mean, then, is that, intrinsically, academic success is more precious than athletic stardom, but acceptance by the peer group is preferable to both, especially during adolescence. And if athletic skills offer a better key to social acceptability, the teen-ager should by all means concentrate on them.

Plausible as it may seem that parents are concerned more about social than academic success for their children there is no real basis for such an assumption. Coleman's findings cannot prove that parents defer to their teen-agers' pursuit of social acceptance by age-mates and encourage them to excel in whatever manner will help them attain that goal. On the contrary, the parents in his study explicitly rated popularity much lower than academic brilliance. It is altogether possible that the adults hypocritically voiced an opinion that was not their own but which they thought more proper to espouse. Or perhaps the students thought wishfully, though erroneously, that their parents supported their dreams for athletic stardom.

Whatever the division or congruence of values between adult and adolescent worlds may be, one fact seems clear: Not only do teen-agers regard success in sports as a more desirable accomplishment than success at school, but they also feel (or at least would like to believe) that their parents support these convictions. It would be interesting to determine if teen-agers think these opinions are shared also by their teachers and society at large.

[6] J. S. Coleman, *Social Climates in High Schools,* Cooperative Research Monograph No. 4 (Washington, D.C.: U.S. Office of Education, 1961).

Reactions to Effort at School and Athleticism

Although academic brilliance and average ability were rated about equal as independent qualities, there was no question about the choice of nonstudiousness over studiousness. Except for the Connecticut populations, most teen-agers canvassed in this study felt that conforming to general practice in the amount of time spent on school work is definitely more acceptable than deviating toward excess. However, these findings offer no hint as to whether the respondents thought diligence at homework should be kept at a minimum or at a moderate level. What they may believe is that study outside of school is not helpful toward building good social relationships no matter how much time is devoted to it, and the greater the time spent, the more precarious are one's chances for social acceptability by peers. On the other hand, the implication may be that serious effort at school is a valued quality among adolescents, more so than indifference to it, but that it should be kept within the bounds of conformity. If so, there follows the danger of the teen-ager's urge toward success at school (and in noneducational endeavors as well) often running counter to his need to maintain nonconspicuous principles and conduct. Academic self-betterment through hard work at school may be a most desirable goal provided it does not "take too much out of you," particularly in isolation from the peer group. Academic ambition is a virtue, but it must be tempered with restraint, and this may give rise to confusion as to the dividing line between diligence and overindulgence and between moderation and lethargy.

Without minimizing its conformity implications, preference for nonstudiousness should also be interpreted on its own merits. The amount of time customarily spent on school assignments may be seen by students and teachers alike as sufficient for achievement at any level. Excessive preoccupation could thus be regarded both as unnecessary for success at school and intrusive on time and energy that might otherwise be directed toward nonscholastic interests. Therefore, the studious person risks being dubbed a "grind" not simply because he is a deviant but because he has budgeted his time unwisely and has funneled most of his efforts into a narrow range of interests when a normal amount of dedication could also bring him average or even outstanding success at school. These considerations may have played a crucial role in the higher rating of nonstudiousness in most schools surveyed and in the higher ranking of the nonstudious characters by the graduate students of education, as noted earlier.

One of the nonscholastic activities definitely valued by adolescents in this study is athletic-mindedness. Its curative power over social ills seems to suggest that the one possessing it can afford certain risks in behavior that may not be tolerated ordinarily. The brilliant–studious person especially stands to gain by taking cognizance of the immunities against social rejection that interest in sports seems to ensure. Certainly, he is more vulnerable to derision from peers than are most students if his attitude toward athletics is thought to be indifferent.

Unlike the ability attributes which are descriptive of status rather than behavior, those referring to effort and athleticism hint at the social orientation of the stimulus character. Studiousness is most often practiced alone, whereas its counterpart may be perceived as freeing the individual to socialize with age-mates. Participation in sports is generally a group activity, while abstention may denote indifference to shared experiences. This suggests the possibility that social-mindedness functioned as a basic criterion by which the stimulus characters were evaluated. Most respondents may have reacted to effort and athleticism not only in terms of the surface attractiveness of these personal qualities, but also in terms of how much they facilitate group activity. Academic brilliance or average ability, on the other hand, could not be judged on this basis, which may account in part for the lack of preference between them.

Group participation, then, is an important ritual in the adolescent world. Teen-agers strive to be socially acceptable by being sociable, and this creates the impression that herdlike activity prevails much of the time. The "lone wolf" may be admired for any number of reasons, but is not necessarily accorded high status unless he contributes to group goals and brings the locus of his activity close to it. One way for such a person to guarantee his own high status among peers is by distinguishing himself in athletics. This kind of personal excellence is popular because it paves the way to group success. Although smashing a home run is an individual rather than collective feat, it is mainly for the star's help to the team that he is idolized. The larger group identifies itself closely with the team through victory and defeat, and the performance of any one player is regarded as part of a cooperative effort even if he carries the team on his shoulders.

What also helps the athletic star become the darling of so wide an audience, even though he is a deviant of sorts, is the fact that his type of brilliance is comprehensible enough to have mass appeal. Most teen-agers can appreciate the inordinate skill required in producing a game-winning home run in the ninth inning or a tie-breaking last-minute touchdown. A comparable feat in theoretical physics can only be understood by a handful of scholars. Being thus out of touch with the larger group, the academic giant may never become as popular a hero as his athletic counterpart,

The fact that stardom in athletics has an amusement and excitement value reaching out to far more spectators than do feats of academic "magic" raises doubts that both kinds of activity can be popularized to the same extent. Yet some writers insist that interscholastic competition in activities of the mind would create widespread enthusiasm, if well advertised. Coleman, for example, asserts that "if there were systematically organized games, tournaments, and meets in all activities ranging from mathematics and English through home economics and industrial arts to basketball and football, and if promotional skills were used, the resulting public interest and student interest in these activities would undoubtedly increase sharply."[7] Is it indeed as simple as that? Can a poetry contest match the thrills generated by a football game? Perhaps for some, but these would have to be a select few connoisseurs rather than the general public or school population, most of whom cannot distinguish between excellence and mediocrity in this field. In areas such as science and mathematics, only those students who are themselves superior can appreciate the brainpower that goes into problem-solving at advanced levels. They may be inspired by well-planned, well-promoted group competition, but they cannot expect many others to go along with their enthusiasm.

Aside from the appeal of athletics to all age groups, adolescents have a special reason for reveling in such activities. To them sports symbolize physical strength, coordination, and maturity, sure signs of approaching adulthood during this transitional stage in their growth. They are conscious of the human physique as a thing of beauty and power, and whoever can shine on the ball field is in effect putting it on display for all to admire. Soundness of body apparently means more to this group than excellence of mind, which could account for the greater admiration of physical strength and agility than mental gymnastics.

TRAITS TYPIFYING THE CHARACTERS

The global score is a composite of ratings on various individual traits and represents some measure of social acceptability. By noting the traits distinctively associated and unassociated with each character, some notion of the characters' individualities is also brought to light. It is thus possible to obtain a "qualitative" impression of the manner in which the imaginary high school students were perceived.

The desirable and undesirable traits were classified separately as "social," "intellectual," "task-related," "personal-emotional," and "school-

[7] J. S. Coleman, *The Adolescent Society* (Glencoe, Illinois: Free Press, 1961), p. 322.

related" (see Tables 3 and 4). Only the trait "popular" was not categorized so that it could be viewed separately in its degree of association with each of the characters. In order to determine the extent to which a trait was regarded as typical of a particular character an inspection was made of how frequently the respondents associated that trait with the given character. As indicated earlier, the students had voted "yes" if they felt the trait typified the character, or "no" if they believed it did not. The total number of "no" responses was then subtracted from the total number of "yes" responses for the trait as it applied to that character, thus indicating how characteristic it was thought to be of him. So, for example, the number of "yes" votes for the trait "popular," as applied to the brilliant–nonstudious athlete, exceeded the number of "no" votes by 444. On the other hand there were 294 more "no" than "yes" votes for the same trait as it referred to the brilliant–studious nonathlete. For each trait, the eight characters were ranked from 1 to 8 in terms of the frequency with which it was associated with them. In the case of the trait "popular," the brilliant–nonstudious athlete ranked highest, which means the trait was regarded most often as typifying him, while the brilliant–studious nonathlete ranked lowest, as indicated by his having received the lowest score for that trait.

Global Scores and Ratings on Special Traits

One striking outcome of this survey was that all characters received positive global scores. A majority of respondents thought most desirable traits personified the characters (hence the greater number of plus scores in Table 3) and most undesirable traits ought not to be associated with them (hence the greater number of minus scores in Table 4.) Yet some characters attracted the trait "popular" fewer times than it was denied them. The teen-agers seemed to be saying that a person can have many admirable qualities or be devoid of many unacceptable ones, and yet remain unpopular among his peers. Perhaps one personal deficiency, be it serious enough, can outweigh much that is laudable when popularity is at stake. Whatever lay behind the respondents' reasoning, it is clear that "social acceptability," as reflected in the global score, was not considered synonymous with "popularity." If the precise ingredients of social acceptability were to be labeled and weighed in this instance one would first have to determine the kinds of emotional reactions evoked by each of the 54 traits. Included among the reactions that added up to a high global score might have been feelings of admiration, envy, affection, and possibly even pity, all of which do not always contribute to popularity. The tendency toward positive ratings on a majority of the traits may also reflect a general inclination to react favorably to an individual even when one feels neutral or uninformed about him in terms of these traits.

In the trait scores there was a general inclination to associate with the characters certain traits which were actually, or by inference, imbedded in the stimulus characteristics. This was especially obvious in traits attached to the athletic and the brilliant characters. The athletes were far ahead of the others in physical traits as well as such traits as "competitive" and "well-rounded," which might well go along with being sports-minded. They were also least likely to be dubbed as "all work, no play" and "doesn't have much fun." The brilliant characters scored well on the desirable school-related traits but were also most likely to attract undesirable ones in this category, such as "teacher's pet" and "brags about marks."

This "return" of "given" information was expected, and it supported the reliability of the instrument. Substantially unexpected, however, was the halo effect surrounding athletic-mindedness. Every athlete attained a higher score than any of the nonathletes on such farfetched traits as "a good conversationalist," "kind," "sociable," "can take responsibility," "mature," " takes criticism well," "a good school citizen," and "pleasing personality." Teen-agers would be hard put to justify a logical relationship between athletic-mindedness and any of these traits; still, interest and participation in sports seem to inspire more virtues than meet the naked eye. Conversely, the stigma of being a nonathlete was carried to curious extremes, as such characters tended to rate higher than any of the athletes on such irrelevant traits as "shy," "doesn't care for the opposite sex," "nervous," and "talks behind your back." This illustrates how one influential characteristic can produce a chain of enhancing or deprecating inferences. Those who are quick to generalize about a person without assembling and weighing facts may be as prone to idolize as to condemn. In either direction the single influential attribute brings on supporting impressions that are apparently neither relevant nor substantiated.

Differences in Trait Associations among Characters

In order to illustrate the qualitative differences between stimulus characters, those ranked successively in mean global scores were compared in terms of traits distinctively associated with them. Comparisons were made between the character attracting the highest global score with the one ranked second, the third with the fourth, the fifth with the sixth, and the seventh with the eighth. Except for those ranked seventh and eighth, none of the comparisons involved characters differing significantly in mean global scores. Yet the differences are marked when one considers the specific traits associated and unassociated with each of the characters (see Tables 3 and 4).

Brilliant–nonstudious–athletic vs. average–nonstudious–athletic. Although both these stimulus characters rated near-equal on the trait "popu-

TABLE: 3: Scores[a] and Ranks[b] Ascribed by the Total Population to the Eight Stimulus Characters for Each Desirable Trait (N=615)

Desirable Traits	Brilliant-Nonstudious-Athletic		Average-Nonstudious-Athletic		Average-Studious-Athletic		Brilliant-Studious-Athletic		Brilliant-Nonstudious-Nonathletic		Average-Nonstudious-Nonathletic		Average-Studious-Nonathletic		Brilliant-Studious-Nonathletic	
	Score	Rank	Score	Rank	Score	Rank	Score	Rank	Score	Rank	Score	Rank	Score	Rank	Score	Rank
Popular	444	1	443	2	255	4	270	3	-53	6	11	5	-153	7	-294	8
Physical traits																
Nice looking	310	2	407	1	260	3	238	4	65	6	144	5	14	7	-142	8
Healthy	479	3	516	1	487	2	471	4	338	6	373	5	320	7	184	8
Dresses well	395	1	357	2	346	3	337	4	239	5	169	6	142	7	132	8
Social traits																
Good sport	483	3	502	1	485	2	438	4	-125	7	-79	6	-70	5	-274	8
Good conversationalist	460	1	293	3	273	4	432	2	232	5	4	7	-26	8	137	6
Good leader	423	1	283	3	157	4	394	2	-19	5	-263	8	-256	7	-164	6
Kind	435	2	438	1	428	3	421	4	270	7	334	6	359	5	202	8
Sociable	460	2	483	1	351	3	349	4	84	6	170	5	0	7	-176	8
Good manners	468	2	394	6	449	3	471	1	436	4	280	8	391	7	396	5
Intellectual traits																
Bright	499	1	139	5	105	6	484	3	492	2	-114	8	-51	7	479	4
Has good ideas	470	2	266	6	291	5	473	1	387	3	8	8	125	7	355	4
Expresses self well	452	2	173	6	185	5	461	1	366	3	-112	8	4	7	347	4
General task-related traits																
Can take responsibility	461	1	312	4	375	3	457	2	290	5	22	8	115	7	280	6
Competitive	342	2	229	4	282	3	367	1	-46	6	-320	8	-167	7	72	5
Conscientious	307	3	24	7	269	4	385	2	259	5	-192	8	256	6	388	1
Obedient	378	4	273	7	388	3	439	1	336	5	176	8	323	6	392	2
Personal-emotional traits																
Mature	398	2	308	4	345	3	405	1	187	5	42	8	115	7	116	6
Cheerful	431	2	456	1	371	3.5	371	3.5	79	6	200	5	5	7	-152	8
Open-minded	346	2	104	5	175	3	376	1	170	4	-97	8	-34	7	79	6
Well-rounded life	422	1	363	2	257	4	294	3	-105	5	-122	6	-233	7	-302	8
Pleasing personality	438	2	448	1	404	3	368	4	126	6	158	5	38	7	-113	8
Takes criticism well	193	3	199	1.5	199	1.5	191	4	-43	6	-52	7	-39	5	-150	8
School-related traits																
Good school citizen	497	2	413	4	464	3	504	1	153	6	28	8	156	5	136	7
Proud of school work	439	4	-46	7	117	5	490	2	446	3	-189	8	42	6	502	1
Has good study habits	286	3	-80	7	252	5	480	1	277	4	-237	8	187	6	452	2
Likes school	391	3	85	7	203	5	450	2	335	4	-236	8	100	6	454	1

TABLE 4: Scores[a] and Ranks[b] Ascribed by the Total Population to the Eight Stimulus Characters for Each Undesirable Trait (N=615)

Undesirable Traits	Brilliant-Nonstudious-Athletic		Average-Nonstudious-Athletic		Average-Studious-Athletic		Brilliant-Studious-Athletic		Brilliant-Nonstudious-Nonathletic		Average-Nonstudious-Nonathletic		Average-Studious-Nonathletic		Brilliant-Studious-Nonathletic	
	Score	Rank	Score	Rank	Score	Rank	Score	Rank	Score	Rank	Score	Rank	Score	Rank	Score	Rank
Social traits																
Creep	-481	7	-531	8	-468	6	-375	5	-155	2	-351	4	-238	3	85	1
Stuck-up	-336	4	-457	7.5	-457	7.5	-258	3	-146	2	-416	6	-346	5	-2	1
Dull	-453	7	-495	8	-395	6	-369	5	-117	4	-208	4	-115	2	104	1
Shy	-452	8	-451	7	-325	5	-350	6	-150	3	-214	4	5	2	35	1
Can't get a date	-360	7	-362	8	-291	6	-262	5	-109	3	-203	4	-45	2	118	1
Doesn't care for opposite sex	-360	7	-372	8	-345	6	-290	5	-159	3	-288	4	-148	2	30	1
Talks about you behind your back	-375	7	-370	6	-377	8	-336	5	-230	3	-179	1	-224	4	-183	2
Intellectual traits																
Walking dictionary	-125	4	-534	7	-503	6	9	3	47	2	-559	8	-483	5	264	1
Bookworm	-364	6	-536	7	-326	5	-37	2	-125	3	-545	8	-171	4	383	1
General task-related traits																
Perfectionist	-109	4	-432	7	-219	6	268	2	-33	3	-490	8	-213	5	339	1
Personal-emotional traits																
Spoiled	-409	6	-491	8	-462	7	-352	3	-178	2	-377	4	-382	5	-115	1
Nervous	-446	7	-451	8	-338	5	-367	6	-273	3	-314	4	-79	1	-101	2
Has answer for every question	-124	4	-377	7	-328	5	36	2	30	3	-400	8	-352	6	170	1
Doesn't have much fun	-383	7	-384	8	-301	6	-289	5	-85	3	-187	4	23	2	168	1
School-related traits																
Teacher's pet	-113	4	-482	7	-413	6	69	2	49	3	-488	8	-347	5	245	1
Brags about marks	-278	4	-431	7	-399	6	-129	3	18	2	-439	8	-312	5	174	1
Complains about never knowing enough	-279	6.5	-360	8	-152	5	-100	4	-89	2	-279	6.5	-93	3	138	1
Dislikes kids who get high marks	-415	8	-261	5	-203	4	-332	7	-273	6	-89	2	-12	1	-161	3
All work, no play	-456	7	-505	8	-409	5	-341	4	-133	3	-432	6	-1	2	310	1

[a] Based on the number of "yes" responses minus the number of "no" responses.
[b] Based on highest to lowest score per trait for the eight stimulus characters.

55

lar," and attracted about equal mean global scores, they were seen as basically different personalities. The brilliant character in this case was more likely to draw the traits commending him for his mental ability, dependability, and high morale with respect to school life. On the other hand, the average-ability character was less susceptible to unattractive traits denoting excessive preoccupation with scholastic activity and arrogance growing out of academic accomplishment. In other words, the brilliant character seems forced to take the bitter with the sweet, for he is not only admired for his ability but also draws invidious epithets because of it. Averageness apparently has the advantage of "nothing ventured, nothing lost." It is interesting to note also that not only did both characters rate highest on global scores, but were regarded most often as "popular."

Brilliant–studious–athletic vs. average–studious–athletic. Here again the difference between brilliant and average characters may be seen in traits denoting ability, responsibility, and pride in school work. The more desirable traits embodying these qualities were associated with the brilliant character but not with his average-ability counterpart. However, the former was also seen as possessing such undesirable traits as "stuck-up," "brags about marks," "has an answer for every question," "talks about you behind your back," "perfectionist," "spoiled," "bookworm," "teacher's pet," and "walking dictionary." None of the undesirable traits was closely associated with the average-ability character; yet he was regarded the less popular of the two. Certainly, he was less spectacular, attracting neither sharp praise nor censure.

Brilliant–nonstudious–nonathletic vs. average–nonstudious–nonathletic. While not differing significantly in mean global scores, these characters were perceived as quite unlike each other. Although the respondents gave slight acknowledgment to the mental advantage enjoyed by the brilliant character, they were far more apt to criticize him as a self-adulating, uninteresting person who seems to be missing out on the variety of life's joys. Unlike his average-ability counterpart, he was regarded by the majority as not "popular" and given little credit for his brains. Pathetic, too, though not as unpopular, was the average–nonstudious nonathlete. No desirable traits were distinctively associated with him, but neither were any undesirable ones. He was viewed as an undistinguished person, drawing neither criticism nor adulation, essentially weak in those attributes that show a sense of responsibility, accomplishment, and varied social interests. In short, the respondents reacted lukewarmly to the average–nonstudious characteristics in combination, showing no really strong emotions either way.

Brilliant–studious nonathletic vs. average–studious–nonathletic. Here we deal with the only two nonathletes whose mean global scores differ significantly. It is therefore noteworthy that the brilliant character, rating lower, actually seemed to fare better than his average-ability counterpart on the desirable traits. The respondents expressed appreciation for his being endowed with brains and for the devotion he shows toward school work. His study habits were lauded more emphatically than were those of the average-ability character, despite the fact that the latter was likewise described as studious and nonathletic. However, the big difference in reactions that rendered the brilliant–studious nonathlete appreciably less acceptable could be seen in the undesirable traits. Many more of these traits were associated with the brilliant than with the average-ability character. The average–studious nonathlete was perceived as the second least acceptable of the eight characters apparently because he was less apt to possess *desirable* traits than were the others. The brilliant character, on the other hand, was rated lowest seemingly because *undesirable* traits were so frequently associated with him. Both were rarely perceived as "popular," and both earned the lowest global scores, the average-ability character for the good qualities he lacked, and the brilliant character for the bad qualities he possessed.

Teachers will regard with interest some of the specific reactions to the brilliant–studious nonathlete. Although the least popular of the eight characters by a wide margin, and although his global score was significantly lower than any of the others, he nevertheless rated highest on such positive traits as "proud of school work," "likes school," and "conscientious." However, he was at the same time unfortunate enough to have all but five of the undesirable traits associated with him by a majority of respondents. From a general inspection of trait scores it would seem that positive attitudes toward school are looked upon with favor, but have no salutary effect on popularity or social acceptance in the adolescent world.

Designation of Stimulus Character as "Boy," "Girl," or "Either"

When the male and female respondents were asked to designate the sex of each of the eight characters by checking "boy," "girl," or "either," it was apparent that the impressions of the two groups differed sharply (see Appendix C, Tables 8 and 9). Whereas the males tended to view the characters more often as "boys" than as "girls" or "either," the females were more apt to regard them as belonging to either sex. There was a greater tendency for the athletes to be perceived by both sexes as boys than were the nonathletes. Also, the stimulus character most often seen as a girl by the males was the brilliant–studious nonathlete, who was also rated lowest in mean global score. Although only about one fifth of the male respondents designated this character as a girl, there may be an implied inclination to associate effeminate qualities with the outstanding student who works hard to accomplish his success but who isolates himself from the vigorous physical activities of youth. Here again, the old claim that intellectualism per se and effeminacy go together is not necessarily supported by the attitudes expressed in this survey. Instead, only when academic brilliance is combined with studiousness and lack of interest in sports do male adolescents, at least, show some tendency toward making such associations.

RELATIONSHIP BETWEEN BACKGROUND FACTORS AND ATTITUDES

An effort was made to test the degree of relationship between character ratings and the respondents' own academic abilities as well as the educational accomplishments of their parents. For the most part, correlations hovered around zero (see Appendix C, Table 10), indicating that for the population studied, the value of information on intelligence and levels of parental education in predicting character ratings was negligible.

The absence of a significant correlation between ratings of the stimulus characters and the aforementioned background variables is one of the most significant outcomes of the study. This finding was a surprise in that it showed a reluctance on the part of respondents to identify themselves sympathetically with the characters they resembled most. Instead, attitudinal conformity was the rule. Even in the case of the brilliant–studious nonathlete, rated significantly lower than any of the others, there was no evidence of a higher regard shown by those who might identify more closely with this character on the basis of ability and dedication to school work.

These data suggest the existence of a melting pot of opinion toward success at school in a setting where youth represent all levels of ability and all shades of educational outlook. It seems that those rating high academically and coming from homes most likely to venerate schooling were prone to express no more positive feelings toward imaginary students nearly like themselves than did their less-endowed peers. Like their schoolmates, they appeared not to regard academic brilliance as an enhancing quality and conceded its possible stigmatic effects upon the reputations of some. What may have operated here was the minority acceptance of attitudes directed at it by the majority, a phenomenon sometimes found in intergroup relations. Borg's study of attitudes toward artists revealed that the latter group tended also to believe in the commonly expressed verbal stereotypes.[8] Cultural minorities, such as Jews and Negroes, were likewise found to exhibit patterns of self-hatred reminiscent of the hostility felt toward these groups by outsiders. Still more closely related to the present results may be those of Seeman's study,[9] in which college professors expressed feelings of shame and indignation regarding intellectuals in general.

If self-rejection was indeed an operative factor in these results, one would have to assume that the academically superior respondents recognized themselves in at least one of several character descriptions, mainly those including brilliance as an attribute. Only then would it seem that the gifted reacted to high school students like themselves in a manner similar to the way the nongifted reacted. However, there is no way to determine whether or not the characters were seen as mirrorlike images for any live teen-agers. Although some specific information was offered about the characters' relative standing in class, they were not vivid enough to be regarded as more than stereotypes that may have reminded the reader of other adolescents rather than of himself. It is therefore impossible to conclude with complete assurance that the near-zero correlations between intelligence and ratings of the brilliant characters represent an out-group acceptance of in-group prejudices. Even where modesty is not an inhibiting factor, "brilliant student" is an appellation ascribed to others rather than to oneself. Those who deserve it may not often be likely to flaunt it.

As for the failure of levels of parental education to predict reactions to the brilliant characters, this may be explained in part by the special nature of the population studied. During the testing sessions, a sizable number of respondents remarked that their parents were foreign born, and their formal education had been curtailed when they emigrated to this country. There is no way of determining how many such cases existed, but for many students the highest level of schooling reached by their parents may have been a poor index of the value placed on formal study by the home. Moreover, the poorly educated among predominantly Jewish immigrant parents could be as desirous of their children's success at school and as respectful of learning as the more highly schooled adults. The extent to which the absence of a correlation between parental education and the

[8] W. R. Borg, "The Effect of Personality and Contact upon a Personality Stereotype," *Journal of Educational Research*, Vol. 49 (1955), pp. 289–294.

[9] M. Seeman, "The Intellectual and the Language of Minorities," *American Journal of Sociology*, Vol. 64 (1958), pp. 25–35.

offspring's attitudes toward academic brilliance may be attributable to an unrepresentative population is a matter of conjecture. However, one should not overlook an important hypothesis implicit in these results, namely, that parents' predisposition to long years of schooling is not necessarily a guarantee of more accepting attitudes toward academic brilliance among their offspring.

In general the expected higher ratings of academic brilliance by the predominantly Jewish population in the New York City high school did not emerge in these results. The faculty representative of the school who assisted in administering the questionnaire was convinced that exceptionally positive attitudes would be expressed by his students because of their Jewish background and values, and that such attitudes would not be typical of the feelings of adolescents elsewhere. Such was not the case, however. Ratings of academic brilliance in comparison to average ability were the same in every community surveyed, despite the fact that the various populations were wide apart in ethnic, social, and religious backgrounds. It would seem, therefore, that reverence for schooling, traditionally associated with the Jewish people, is not translated into higher personal regard for the academically superior by Jewish teen-agers. They may be more convinced than most other adolescents that success at school is a precious objective, but the lure of acceptance by peers seems not to be one of the factors strengthening this conviction. Perhaps among Jewish students scholastic excellence is more popular and desirable than the schoolmate who personifies it.

REACTIONS OF MALES AND FEMALES

Several sharp contrasts can be seen in the reactions of the sexes to the eight stimulus characters (see Figure 9). Immediately apparent is the difference in ranges of mean global scores. Although both groups rated brilliant–nonstudious–athletic highest and brilliant–studious–nonathletic lowest, the mean global score ascribed to the top-ranked character by the female respondents was 31.4 as against 25.3 by the males; the mean global score for the character ranked last was 1.6 by the females and 2.8 by the males. Evidently, the reactions tended to be more extreme among the females than among males.

A comparison of mean differences in character ratings by the sexes helps clarify where the reactions diverged. Whereas both sexes rated every athlete significantly higher than any of the nonathletes, the girls were more discriminating than the boys within both the athlete and nonathlete categories. There were no significant differences among ratings of

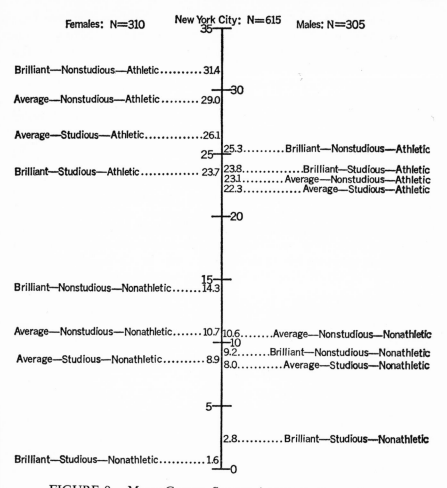

FIGURE 9. MEAN GLOBAL SCORES ASCRIBED BY THE SEXES
TO THE EIGHT STIMULUS CHARACTERS

athletes by the males; among the nonathletes only the brilliant–studious character was scored significantly lower than any of the other three, which did not differ from each other. The females, on the other hand, differentiated more among both the athletes and nonathletes. Although they rated the top-ranked brilliant–nonstudious athlete and the second-ranked average–nonstudious athlete about equal, both characters were rated significantly higher than either of the two studious athletes. Moreover, the average–studious athlete, ranked third by the females, rated significantly better than the fourth-ranked brilliant–studious athlete. As for the nonathletic characters, the females differentiated not only between the brilliant–studious and each of the other nonathletes, as did the males, but they also rated the brilliant–nonstudious one significantly better than the average–nonstudious one.

Illuminating differences in the reactions of males and females may be found in a comparison of mean global scores ascribed separately by the sexes to each of the eight characters (see Appendix C, Table 2). Four of the eight comparisons proved significant at or beyond the .05 level, and in each of these instances the females' rating was higher than the males'. The four characters favored by the females were the brilliant–nonstudious–athletic, the average–nonstudious–athletic, the average–studious–athletic, and the brilliant–nonstudious–nonathletic. These characters were divided evenly between brilliant and average, but three out of the four were nonstudious and three out of the four were athletic, thus revealing that the females tended to be more attracted to nonstudiousness and sportsmindedness than were the males.

RATINGS OF CHARACTERISTICS SINGLY AND IN COMBINATION

Analyses of reactions to the three stimulus characteristics, *ability, effort,* and *athleticism,* show basic agreement between the sexes in the sense that boys and girls had no preference between brilliance and average ability but both preferred nonstudiousness and athletic-mindedness among the *effort* and *athleticism* stimuli (see Appendix C, Tables 5 and 6). Important disagreements between the sexes were found, however, in their attitudes toward combinations of characteristics. Although the interaction of *ability* and *effort* proved nonsignificant to the male population, it was significant for the females (see Appendix C, Tables 5 and 6). Figure 10 further clarifies these differences. It shows that whereas females did not differentiate significantly between pairs of brilliant and average *nonstudious* characters, among the *studious* they rated the average significantly higher than the brilliant. The males, on the other hand, rated the pairs of brilliant and average characters near-equal within both the studious and nonstudious groups. In short, the combination of academic brilliance and strong preoccupation with school work seemed to be regarded as particularly unfortunate by the females, not so by the males.

According to the females, the strong effects of *athleticism* per se coupled with the relative weakness of *ability* per se in eliciting positive or negative reactions produced results wholly dependent on the character's athletic-mindedness. With *effort* held constant, the mean scores for pairs of brilliant and average athletes did not differ, and the same lack of dis-

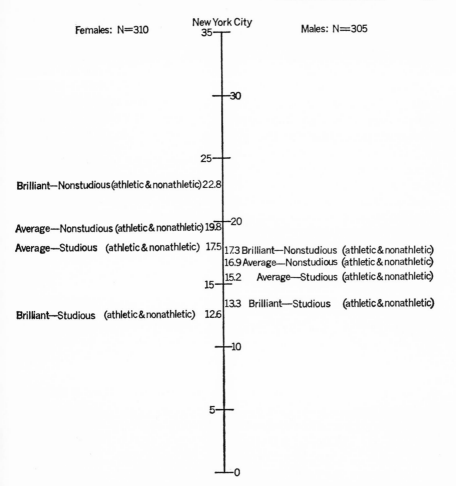

FIGURE 10.   MEAN GLOBAL SCORES ASCRIBED BY THE SEXES
TO PAIRS OF STIMULUS CHARACTERS IDENTICAL IN *Ability*
AND *Effort* BUT OPPOSITE IN *Athleticism*

crimination was shown toward brilliant and average nonathletes (see
Figure 11). Contrasted to these reactions were those of the males who
were influenced by the interaction effects of *ability* and *athleticism* (see
Appendix C, Tables 5 and 6). Whereas pairs of brilliant and average-
ability athletes were rated about equal, the difference in mean scores of
pairs of brilliant and average nonathletes was significant (in favor of the
average). For the males, being brilliant and having no interest in sports
produced especially negative reactions.

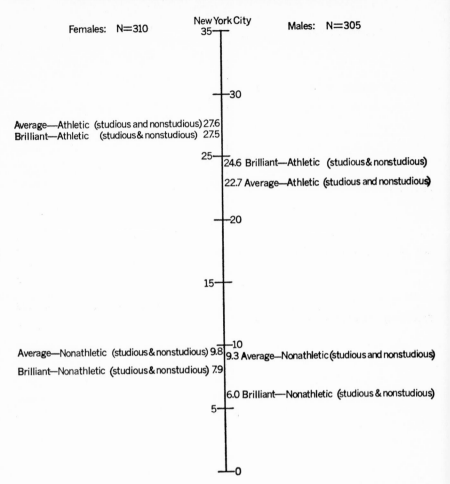

FIGURE 11.   MEAN GLOBAL SCORES ASCRIBED BY THE SEXES
TO PAIRS OF STIMULUS CHARACTERS IDENTICAL IN *Ability*
AND *Athleticism* BUT OPOSITE IN *Effort*

Further disagreement between the sexes was found in their perception
of the interaction effects of *effort* and *athleticism*. Here the females em-
phasized the main effects of the two characteristics while the males were
sensitive to the interaction between them (see Appendix C, Tables 5 and
6). The females differentiated separately on the basis of *effort* and
athleticism. Figure 12 shows that they favored pairs of nonstudious
characters significantly over pairs of studious characters both among the
athletes and nonathletes. Similarly, the girls gave the athletes significantly

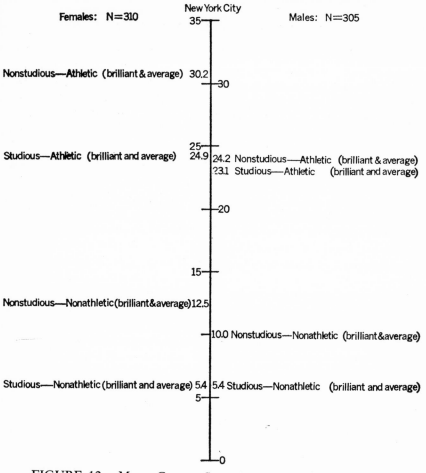

FIGURE 12.   MEAN GLOBAL SCORES ASCRIBED BY THE SEXES
TO PAIRS OF STIMULUS CHARACTERS IDENTICAL IN *Effort*
AND *Athleticism* BUT DIFFERENT IN *Ability*

higher mean scores than the nonathletes regardless of whether they were
all studious or nonstudious. The males, on the other hand, differed with
the females on one comparison of studious and nonstudious pairs of
characters. Although they rated the nonstudious nonathletes significantly
better than the studious nonathletes, they did not discriminate between the
studious and nonstudious athletes. Thus, to the males, a studious character's undesirability depended on his being uninterested in athletics, whereas among the females being studious was relatively unacceptable regardless of the character's sports-mindedness.

INTERPRETATION OF DISAGREEMENTS BETWEEN THE SEXES

As indicated earlier, there was disagreement between the sexes in their ratings of four out of the eight stimulus characters, the females ascribing significantly higher global scores in every case. Of the four characters, two were brilliant and two average; three were nonstudious, one studious; and three were athletic, one nonathletic. Thus, it appears that the females were inclined to regard nonstudiousness and athletic-mindedness more highly than did the males.

Some of the clues as to what may have caused the differences in attitudes are evident in the nature of the population studied. The respondents were high school juniors, only one year away from graduation, and probably beginning to think seriously about the place of education in their future. At this stage of a student's development, decisions with regard to careers and college attendance loom into reality. A definite evaluation of the academic life must then be made. Those who choose a posthigh school education, either out of enthusiasm for scholarly pursuits or out of reluctant acknowledgment of the material reward accruing from advanced study, are compelled by their decision to take a more serious view of the effort needed to succeed in school work than do those for whom secondary education is terminal.

To the extent that feelings about work-mindedness at school are associated with one's educational ambition, there is some basis for attitudinal differences due to sex membership. Evidence shows that despite female superiority over males in high school grades, fewer females than males plan on a college education upon completion of their high school studies. This divergence in outlook, occurring around their junior year at school, may be part of the role realities that attract the females more toward the social aspects of school life and the males more toward academic responsibility. The culture expects girls to relate better to people than to ideas. The ideal wife and homemaker is not perceived as an intellectual giant or even terribly conversant in scholarly matters. More important are such matters as social poise, physical attractiveness, personal efficiency, the ability to provide warm companionship for the mate, and the skills needed to instill in children highly desirable social qualities.

Female high school students prepare well for these adulthood roles. As Coleman[10] revealed in his study, they regard "having a good personality" of paramount importance. Success at school was found to be somewhat helpful in making a girl popular with other girls, but it contributed little if

[10] Coleman, *Social Climates in High Schools, op. cit.*

anything toward her popularity with boys. Moreover, the boy's popularity with girls was related less to doing well in school than to his social success with other boys. Females showed themselves as far more conscious of becoming acceptable to the opposite sex than did the males, and the girls were considerably more sensitive to the problems of not having friends. Perhaps most important, the desire of the brightest female students to be remembered for scholastic achievement declined during their four-year stay in high school, while the brightest male students' desire to be thus remembered increased over that period.

With the girls' respect for academic success waning, and their respect for social success growing as they progress through adolescence, it is perhaps understandable that they were more attracted than the males to nonstudiousness and athletic-mindedness. The nonstudious and athletic characters personify to teen-agers the glamorous figures who make their mark in the social rather than intellectual domain. These characters may qualify for the females' affections because they are the kinds of students who make friends more easily and freely and share adolescents' idealization of sport. The girls, becoming ever more conscious of their sex roles in society, can take greater liberties in maximizing the attractiveness of those who relate to peers and play rather than to study. And since the males are more often forced to continue their education beyond high school and to play the role of the enterprising male, the prospect of hard academic work may be a more acceptable reality to them than to their classmates of the opposite sex who need not make that kind of sacrifice in order to remain on the educational conveyor belt toward success as an adult.

Especially in the school where the present study was conducted, with its large Jewish population, there is reason to believe that males were the more serious-minded about posthigh school education. The middle-class Jewish home shows unusually high respect for schooling but the pressure to go on to college is probably applied more forcefully to males than to females. Not only is the female likely to be offered the choice of terminating her education at the minimum required age; she may also be vulnerable to criticism by parents and peers if she relinquishes opportunities to socialize in favor of preoccupying herself with book learning. Isolation from social activities can be a handicap, especially for those concerned more about proving themselves good marriage choices than in planning for careers that require advanced educational preparation. Hence, the possibly stronger acceptance of the nonstudious and athletic characters by the social-minded females even in the ethnic group that formed the vast majority of the present population.

Summary of Outcomes and Conclusions

A number of important insights into adolescents' attitudes toward academic brilliance were revealed through the present survey:

1. The adolescents surveyed rated academic brilliance per se about equal to average ability as a personal attribute.

2. The adolescents rated academic brilliance as far less acceptable than average ability in the case where its possessor also devotes a greater-than-average amount of time to schoolwork and lacks interest in sports.

3. Studiousness per se was rated a less acceptable attribute than nonstudiousness in all but one of the communities surveyed.

4. Athletic-mindedness was regarded as far more desirable than its absence.

5. Female adolescents tended to favor nonstudiousness and athletic-mindedness more than did the males.

6. The attitudes expressed toward each of the fictitious characters were not influenced by the respondents' intelligence levels nor by the extent of their parents' education.

Insofar as verbal stereotypes reflect face-to-face relations, these results suggest that academic brilliance in and of itself is not a stigma in the adolescent world. However, when it is combined with relatively unacceptable attributes, it can penalize its possessor severely. The nonstudious athlete may demonstrate outstanding brainpower without fearing social derogation by peers; but a display of brilliance by one who is studious and indifferent to sports constitutes a definite status risk. The implied impression is that the brilliant student is an exceptionally prominent target for teen-age pressures to conform to certain behaviors and values. If so, there is danger of his deliberately masking his talent in order to relieve these pressures.

5

Postscript on Implications

Every researcher in education knows that research is often a two-edged blade. With one edge he can cut deeply and revealingly into unexplored areas of human behavior. With the other he can carve up empirical evidence to fit snugly with his preconceived ideas. The problem of misinterpreting data has plagued many an investigator toiling objectively for the advancement of knowledge. For those with pet doctrines to promote, a little evidence can surely be a dangerous thing.

Studies of interpersonal attitudes have their special brand of pitfalls. A person's feelings toward another may appear disarmingly obvious to the naked eye, though in reality they are kaleidoscopic and elusive. Even a systematic effort at exploring them can be frustrating because one is tempted both to ignore inevitable limitations in research technique and to spin too many inferences from too little material evidence. Since the present study adopted one of several alternative approaches, it would be well to consider its particular strengths and limitations and to suggest some implications growing out of the assembled data that are hopefully not too farfetched.

VERBAL STEREOTYPES AS INDICES OF ATTITUDES

The Meaning of Global Score

Most of the previously discussed results were derived from character ratings, or global scores, representing several dimensions of social acceptability. The ingredients blending into a single score derived for a character include judgments on such varied qualities as leadership, sociability, physical appearance, and personal habits. Some of these attributes are apparently more admirable than endearing; others seem calculated to ensure popularity but not as much respect. The inclusiveness of these elements constitutes the strength of the global score as a measure of rela-

69

tive acceptability. However, taking the "yes" and "no" responses to a wide range of characteristics and reducing them to a single rating invites dangers of oversimplification. One such problem resulted from the lack of information regarding the degree of desirability or undesirability of each trait so that the responses might be weighted accordingly. A "yes" response to the trait "popular" may be a far stronger expression of acceptance than a similar reaction to "competitive," although both were numbered among the desirable traits and each response was rated equally ($+1$) in computing the global score. The same is true of the undesirable traits, some of which may be more injurious to one's reputation than others.

Another difficulty posed by the global score concerns the treatment of "no" responses to the various traits. Since a -1 score was assigned to rejection of desirable traits as typifying a given character and a $+1$ to rejection of undesirable traits, there is an implied assumption that the absence of an enhancing quality in a person is necessarily a defect and that there is as much virtue in lacking a disapproved trait as there is in possessing an acceptable one. A "yes" response to "shy," for example, denotes a negative reaction because this trait is regarded as undesirable and therefore detracts from the character's reputation. Does this mean that the lack of shyness adds to one's appeal? To regard the absence of a negative attribute as additive in this sense seems somewhat paradoxical; yet it is precisely what was done in the scoring of such a response.

A basically similar question may be raised with respect to the equivalence of a "no" response to a desirable trait and a "yes" response to an undesirable one. Since either type of reaction is rated -1, the possibility is overlooked that possession of a personal defect may often be perceived more negatively than the absence of a virtue. Moreover, there is nothing in the scoring system to take into account the fact that an unacceptable attribute may cancel the salutary effects of more than one desirable trait. These are important considerations in view of the differences between brilliant and average stimulus characters in terms of the specific trait ratings each received. The brilliant characters tended to have undesirable traits more often associated with them than did their average-ability counterparts. If possession of negative qualities is indeed indicative of exceptionally serious personal failings, the differences in attitudes toward the two kinds of imaginary teen-agers may be more dramatic than is now apparent from the global scores. The brilliant characters who seem more prone to possess undesirable traits may in reality be unable to compensate for these defects through their superior ratings on the desirable traits, at least to the extent that they do under the global scoring system. This is especially worthy of attention since there are unequal numbers of desirable and undesirable traits, with eight fewer of the latter type on the total list.

Finally, there is the problem of combining into a single score the separate reactions to 54 traits, each of which was rated out of context. To be "nice looking" may be desirable under all circumstances, but can the same be said for the trait "conscientious"? The student who spends more time on homework than do most of his schoolmates is surely regarded as conscientious, but it is precisely this characteristic that penalizes him in his relations with peers, for his diligence is applied in the "wrong" area of activity. Demonstrated on the athletic field, however, conscientiousness may be considered an admirable quality. For certain traits, therefore, desirability depends on the situations in which they are revealed and on the kinds of other personal qualities they modify. Nevertheless, they were scored uniformly in the present study. The rigidity of this system of rating also created an ambiguous situation in which "yes" responses to some undesirable traits necessitated similar reactions to desirable ones. For example, the imaginary character perceived as one who "brags about his (her) marks" had to be regarded also as one who is "proud of his (her) school work," the first response being scored -1 and the other $+1$, thus failing in combination to reflect the true negative feeling expressed toward the character.

The various limitations of the global score as indicating the degree of character acceptability suggest that it be interpreted in a relative rather than absolute sense. It would be naïve, for example, to conclude that all stimulus characters were perceived positively from the fact that none had a negative mean global score. A more precise measure would be needed to determine this. However, the global score is appropriate for making comparisons among the stimulus characters through a single rating that is based on a wide variety of criteria. Since one of the major purposes of the study was to investigate the acceptability of the characters relative to each other, a general comprehensive measure was deemed most efficient for realizing this aim. Therein lies the advantage in the use of the global score.

Implications for Predicting Face-to-face Relationships

A basic consideration in interpreting the character ratings is that of determining how predictive they are of reactions to live individuals who fill the same or similar description. Upon this fundamental issue rests the practical application of the present results toward clarifying adolescent feelings about academically brilliant peers. To some extent the practicality of the findings is contaminated by the possible difficulty in locating persons about whom all would agree as resembling any of the stimulus characters. However, even in cases where such agreement exists, the question arises as to what degree the attitudes expressed through the ascription of verbal stereotypes correspond with those communicated in face-to-face encounters.

Several writers have theoretically classified components of intergroup attitudes, and the relationship among those components is relevant to the question at hand. Harding, Kutner, Proshansky, and Chein[1] identified three such elements, the cognitive, affective, and conative. The *cognitive* embraces the various perceptions, beliefs, and expectations that an individual holds with regard to various social groups. These include the association of stereotypes with a given group but do not enter the question of the extent to which personal interaction or social distance is desired. The *affective* component deals with the over-all feelings toward a particular group, usually expressed in terms of friendliness or hostility. Finally, the *conative* component goes beyond the emotional predispositions and enters the dimension of policy orientation. It is obvious from these descriptions that the present study concerned itself exclusively with the cognitive elements of human attitudes.

A somewhat different formulation of attitude components was developed by Bastide and Vandenberghe and illustrated by Guttman as follows:

I. Stereotype: *Belief* of (a White subject) that *his own group* (excels - does not excel) in *comparison* with Negroes on (desirable traits).

II. Norm: *Belief* of (a White subject) that *his own group* (ought - ought not) *interact* with Negroes in (social ways).

III. Hypothetical interaction: *Belief* of (a White subject) that he *himself* (will - will not) *interact* with Negroes in (social ways).

IV. Personal interaction: *Overt action* of (a White subject) *himself* (to - not to) *interact* with Negroes in (social ways).[2]

Logically, one would expect the cognitive or stereotype components of attitudes to be weaker predictors of behavior in personal interaction than any of the other elements postulated by Guttman and by Harding, Kutner, Proshansky, and Chein. Guttman reports empirical evidence indicating that the correlations of feeling expressed in personal interaction with those revealed through "stereotype," "norm," and "hypothetical interaction" were .25, .51, and .49, respectively. From these findings, it would

---

[1] J. Harding, B. Kutner, H. Proshansky, and I. Chein, "Prejudice and Ethnic Relations," in G. Lindzey (ed.), *Handbook of Social Psychology* (Cambridge, Massachusetts: Addison-Wesley Press, 1954).

[2] L. Guttman, "A Structural Theory for Intergroup Beliefs and Action," *American Sociological Review,* Vol. 24 (June 1959), p. 319.

seem that a study dealing strictly with verbal stereotypes, such as the present one, cannot obtain information that is strongly indicative of face-to-face attitudes. However, Harding, Kutner, Proshanksy, and Chein apparently disagree, concluding from their review of the literature that "the relationship among the various attitudinal components (e.g., the cognitive, affective, and conative) is so close that it does not make much difference in practice whether we use cognitive, affective, or conative tendencies to rank individuals with respect to their attitudes toward any specific ethnic group."[3]

Keeping in mind the foregoing comments on the general relationship between stereotypical impressions and behavior dispositions, one can proceed to view the present findings in comparison to studies of the sociometric status of the gifted. As indicated in Chapter 2, past research reveals a slight positive correlation between intelligence and friendship choice, at least up to certain high limits of the intelligence scale. It is possible that attitudes assessed by sociometric techniques provide a clearer picture of the individual's behavioral orientation toward a brilliant person than does a study of stereotypes associated with imaginary characters described as academically brilliant. What the former type of study leaves unexplored, however, is the problem of whether or not intelligence per se influences the acceptability ratings. It offers no evidence that reactions are attracted by the individual's ability rather than by any number of other personal qualities correlated with ability but not necessarily brought on by it. For example, socioeconomic standing is known to be associated both with academic and sociometric status,[4] which implies that those with higher IQs may be more acceptable friendship choices not because of their brains but perhaps because they possess the distinctive values and behaviors of the middle and upper classes which they are more likely to represent. In a direct study of face-to-face relationships, it is therefore extremely difficult to control the myriad factors about the individual that makes him more or less attractive to those who judge him.

Where the investigation is designed to deal with stereotypes ascribed to nonexistent but carefully described characters, it is possible to be reasonably sure which elements in the description stimulate the various reactions. The present study achieved its objective by clarifying the main effects of academic brilliance upon adolescent attitudes, as well as the interaction effects of brilliance in combination with other attributes. And since there is a definite relationship—be it great or small—between attitudes revealed through verbal stereotype and those expressed in face-to-

[3] Harding, Kutner, Proshansky, and Chein, *loc. cit.*, p. 1030.
[4] A. B. Hollingshead, *Elmtown's Youth* (New York: John Wiley & Sons, 1949).

face encounter, the present findings help determine the effects of high scholastic status on social acceptability.

Aside from revealing to some extent how academic brilliance is perceived by adolescents in their interpersonal relationships, the results of this study may also be applied to situations where judgments are founded on verbal report rather than on firsthand contact. One well-known example of published descriptions or even caricatures forming a basis for popular decision-making is the case of political candidates running for public office. In everyday life, too, predispositions toward individuals are often established by reactions to verbal reports about them prior to actual encounter. The high school student who is keenly aware of the way descriptions of him can influence attitudes, may be conscious of the need to establish actively an acceptable reputation for himself. If he is gifted, the prospect of being dubbed "brilliant," "studious," and "nonathletic" can cause him to lean over backward in order to avoid fitting this image. This may require hiding his academic lights under a bushel. Or he may regard the necessity to exert only moderate effort at school and to participate in sports as a convenient rationalization for lack of scholastic fulfillment. The mere fact that minimizing academic effort and achievement in order to conform to group behavior may be an available rationalization for poor performance at school is in itself an alarming note deserving dedicated attention.

IMPLICATIONS FOR EDUCATIONAL POLICY AND RESEARCH

People concerned with the educational climate in schools cannot help but note that the results of the present study tend to dispel some popular notions about the valuation of academic brilliance among high school students. Those who feel that educators have generally succeeded in celebrating the academic life for adolescents will find little to substantiate this claim in the expressed attitudes toward high scholastic status. On the other hand, those who are convinced that being brilliant at school inevitably produces social handicaps will also find their views contradicted by the present results. Unequivocal opinions of this kind should be rejected in favor of more subtle and probing analysis. The many assertions regarding rampant anti-intellectualism or cultural revivalism do not provide a clear picture of what actually exists in the school world. What these observations may be revealing are superficial symptoms which, left unexplored in greater depth, can lead to more deception than enlightenment.

More nearly approaching the truth is the finding that there is no special halo over academic accomplishment per se at school. In that fascinating, near-insular world of adolescence, earning good grades can be an added ornament but never the substance of attractiveness. Academic superiority is appreciated in those who have "set their houses in order" by acquiring other personal qualities that really count. Without such fundamental requisites, deviance toward success at school becomes a social liability. Whether the existence of this state of affairs can be attributed to the neglect or design of educators remains open to question.

In the light of these results one might, indeed, ask whether the American high school is actively involved in propagating the life of the mind among our youth. The question may seem fatuous to those who have heard educators claim repeatedly that schools are dedicated to producing an educated citizenry. Still, there is reason to suspect that the typical classroom has not succeeded, or perhaps not shown real interest, in enveloping its students with the thrill of contact with great ideas. One cannot help sensing a reluctance on the part of school officials to influence student career aspirations and ways of life in the direction of scholarliness or creativity. It is as if educators are saying in effect to the student: "We are as pleased with your interest in sports as we would be if you showed a similar thirst for books. All we ask is that while indulging your interests and aptitudes you learn to utilize your basic educational tools for personal enlightenment or vocational attainment." This is quite different from saying: "Our first and foremost service to students is to build intellect. We regard our having fulfilled that function best when we nurture high-level contributors to culture among those with the capacity for it, and also patrons of art and thought among those incapable of making significant contributions. Regardless of what your personal interests and aptitudes may be, we would like to impress on you our feeling that in halls of learning, learning remains supreme. You may not all be able to participate in it on an equally high level, but you ought to respect it, foster it, and somehow become enriched by it."

In a school environment where little effort is made to influence attitudes toward intellect it is not surprising to find, as Coleman[5] did, that the boys in a number of high schools were more eager to become nationally famous athletes or jet pilots than atomic scientists, and that girls favored growing up to be models or nurses rather than schoolteachers or artists. These choices betray the strong influence of mass media which are far more assertive than schools in preaching the "good life" to adults and youth alike. Incidentally, among the most cherished icons built by the mass media are the mass media themselves. Is it not the vague dream of most

[5] J. S. Coleman, *Social Climates in High Schools,* Cooperative Research Monograph No. 4 (Washington, D.C.: U.S. Office of Education, 1961).

adolescent boys and girls to be seen or heard on television, radio, or the stage? The academic spotlight at school is, unfortunately, not nearly as attractive.

Some may believe that the school's relative reserve in glamorizing the ideals of intellectual endeavor is both necessary and appropriate. According to these viewpoints, an education for all children and youth must apply flexibly to fit the needs of students coming from every conceivable social origin and ranging widely in intellectual ability and career aspirations. Inasmuch as only a mere fraction of students can aspire to high-level productivity, educators may regard it as foolhardy to single out the life of the atomic scientist or poet for special attraction.

Yet educational leaders should own up to the fact that in attempting to be all things to all students they have failed to make academic work desirable for its own sake even among those most likely to succeed in it. If preoccupation with ideas is a major institutional goal, the school cannot thus far claim success in having transmitted it to teen-agers. If, on the other hand, nurture of academic excellence is only one of many school objectives, all viewed with equal importance, its pursuit may be vitiated by the diffusion of effort. The encomium for the math whiz loses some of its glitter at school if comparable official honor is lavished on football stars, speed-demon typists, and social butterflies. Granted, there is room for many kinds of champions in our society, but if so many are to be crowned with indiscriminate enthusiasm by the school, it may lose its public image as primarily a patron of intellect and creativity. Much *can* be learned from the mass media which dare to delineate their hero images even though most of the audience is incapable of emulating them. Where, but in our schools, can and should the ideal of the academic life be fashioned?

What follows, then, is the key question of whether adolescent attitudes toward academic brilliance have any bearing on their scholastic performance. Some available evidence suggests that there may be a strong relationship. Of particular significance is Coleman's finding that in schools where students held academic brilliance in relatively low esteem those with the highest IQs were not likely to earn the highest grades. Apparently, outstanding success at school depends relatively less on native ability and more on sheer determination where the status of intellect is low in the student group. The gifted find they must battle apathy or resentment of peers, and many lapse into mediocrity in the belief that they can avoid rejection thereby. Those who possess the necessary drive and doggedness to risk ostracism are not always the highly able. Hence, the prevailing climate of opinion regarding intellectualism may be a valuable gauge of the extent to which students with high potential tend to hide their lights under a bushel.

The possible effects of attitudes on performance are even more readily apparent when the school records of male and female students are compared. Previously noted findings in Coleman's study indicate that girls tend to attach less importance to scholastic endeavor than do boys. Here again, motivation seems to become a relatively greater factor in achievement, while ability plays a comparatively lesser role. Coleman reports that the best male students generally had higher IQs than the most proficient female students. Says he: "These results, together with the earlier ones which show that the girls have better grades than boys, suggest the peculiar dilemma of the girl: She is pushed toward doing well in school by her allegiance to parents and teachers; but if she wants dates and popularity, she is constrained from going all out scholastically. As a consequence, many of the brightest girls manage to hide their brightness, letting somewhat less intelligent girls be named best students."[6]

Since the educational outlooks of high school boys and girls seem to contrast sharply, some interesting questions may be opened with regard to coeducational practices. Perhaps because the idea of coeducation is a relatively recent one in the long history of formal schooling, its effects on motivation and achievement have never been adequately examined. The assumption is often made that permitting boys and girls to be classmates in high school not only preserves equality between the sexes but also has a salutary effect on their social development. That alone is reason enough to justify the practice.

There is certainly no intention here to question the value of coeducation on the basis of previously noted findings on sex differences in attitudes toward intellectual endeavor. It may well be that if healthy boy-girl relations are fostered thereby, this consideration should outweigh all others. What seems indicated, however, is the need for a thoroughgoing study of how coeducation affects the accomplishments of both sexes at school. Such a study would take into account all aspects of growth that may be involved, including the personal, social, and scholastic development of students as well as their vital adult dreams. In what ways do sex roles differ with respect to academic interests and aspirations, and how do the sexes influence each other in a coeducational setting? Would these influences, such as they are, exist even if the boys and girls were separated at school? Do educators place any clear-cut value judgments on the sex roles of American youth so as to determine whether changes in them ought to be made?

Much depends, of course, on the effectiveness of schools in molding student attitudes toward education and intellectuality. Some educators

[6] Coleman, *op cit.*, pp. 49, 50.

may feel that only society at large is responsible for such climates of feeling and the school is too weak to exert much influence one way or the other. Others may believe that the school can control attitudinal currents only through great effort and near-magical formulas. Several school administrators who have looked at the results of the present study have expressed the belief that they can raise the status of their gifted students through skillful use of curricular and cocurricular planning. They are convinced that even though group solidarity among adolescents is strong, the impact of school and community does make a difference.

In the hope that adolescent values are susceptible to adult influence, several important tasks face American educators. There is need to know more about what produces such inflexible group cohesiveness among American youth that the individual's bent often becomes stifled by the need to be acceptable to peers. Why, indeed, is being well liked contingent upon being undistinguished in so many productive ways? Little is gained toward the understanding of teen-agers by terming them rebels against adult society or imperfect reflectors of it and letting it go at that. Much greater probing into the *dynamics* of adolescent group life is required. Only then can the school begin to study how to influence social norms rather than stand by passively as they unfold under influences originating out of school.

Some of the basic tasks facing educational researchers today may, therefore, be summarized as follows:

1. Studies ought to ascertain the extent to which the present findings can be generalized to other school populations. Researchers often tend to describe adolescent society as if it were homogeneous in its values, ignoring the possible existence of local influences and orientations. Evidence from the Connecticut schools surveyed, for example, shows that adolescent attitudes toward industriousness at school is not necessarily the same in every community or even in every school. One reason for sampling a number of school populations is to bring home to educators the fact that any attempt to mold the life of an individual student must take into account the living pattern of the group. The student population is a social unit, complete with its own laws and customs. If there are differences from one setting to the next, it is incumbent on the local educator to know what distinguishes his student group from every other. He should realize that group solidarity is so strong that he may be forced to deal with it as a unit even when he seeks to exert his influence on a single member. To convince a gifted student of the thrill and rewards of a scholarly life would then involve an effort to raise the status of intellectual pursuits among the

entire school population. The excitement of ideas would have to be "in the air" even though all could not participate on the same high level. This implies a radical departure from the one-to-one relationship between educator and student where motivation is usually aimed at the individual without reference to the group rather than at the group which in turn disciplines the individual.

2. A thoroughgoing study of adolescent opinions of academic brilliance is only part of the information gathering responsibilities of educators. Equally important is a clarification of their own attitudes. This means more than merely assessing attitudes as they exist. It involves also hammering out a point of view supported by some clear-cut philosophic underpinnings.

It would be interesting to know the feelings of teachers and administrators about the eight stimulus characters in this study. Although the graduate students of education who ranked the stimulus characters in terms of the kind of students they would prefer to teach showed some favoritism toward the academically brilliant, they also rated athletic-mindedness higher than any other attribute and looked on studiousness with relative disfavor. If the educators had been asked to rate the characters individually in terms of typifying traits, some interesting insights might have emerged. Some would perhaps have viewed the task as that of making a choice between democracy and meritocracy. For exalting the brilliant and stigmatizing the mediocre may be regarded as a form of snobbery as intolerable as intolerance toward intellectuals. However difficult it is to establish a defensible point of view, the educator cannot avoid the difficulty by refusing to take a stand. This kind of neutrality will do nothing for the brilliant student who needs encouragement even though he works hard at school assignments and does not indulge much in play.

3. Before undertaking to initiate change, schools should learn more about what is involved in change induction among adolescents. A better understanding of how representative of society's attitudes were those expressed by the present population would help place the problem in clear perspective. If the kind of negativism expressed toward brilliance in certain kinds of students reflects powerful anti-intellectual leanings rooted in American society, the school's efforts to produce change in students may be doomed to abortion from the outset. A much broader enterprise, encompassing more than the school world, would be necessary.

One important aid to schools in their attempt to influence adolescent values stems from the increasingly important role of youth in the life-and-death struggle of democracy. Brainpower today constitutes a vital political weapon. Headlines have brought this fact home to an alerted nation, and it is inconceivable that our youth has remained unaffected. For once, teen-agers are being made to realize that the adult world does not regard them merely as physically mature people with prolonged childhoods, but instead looks to them as vital hopes for the survival of the nation. Today, it is dangerous to assume a patronizing attitude toward budding talent. The gifted youth and his peers know that he is a precious commodity that adults appreciate. This sense of importance alone can have a profound impact upon adolescent feelings about brains as time goes on and world tensions prevail. Schools should be aware of the possibility of attitudinal change and assess it frequently.

Of course, it is not the business of education merely to allow youthful feelings about scholarliness to be swayed by the temper of the times. The classroom is hopefully the place where attitudes can be forged rather than just reflected. An already existing treasure of classroom techniques can be employed to drive home the importance of thought and creativity. Much can be learned too from the influences that idealize the values of athletic pursuits among teen-agers. Competition, team identity, the promise of immediate and long-term rewards, are well-known conditions in the world of sports that might be applied experimentally in the realm of ideas. Some of the healthiest and most potent techniques used in convincing youth about the desirability of an athletic physique might also help convince them of the beauties of an agile mind. A school that refuses to make the effort toward strengthening incentives toward scholarship and creativity can hardly claim to be carrying out its complete function in society.

Appendix A

Trait Clusters Containing Adjectives and Descriptive Phrases

TRAIT LIST I

Acts big
Big deal
Brags about his (her) marks [a]
Brags about never studying
Conceited
Feels no one can equal him
Feels he is above the average person
False sense of modesty
Humble
Haughty
"I am better than you" attitude
Know-it-all attitude
Looks down upon others
Not egotistical
"No one else is as good" attitude
Snobbish
Stuck-up [a]
Shows off his (her) brilliance
Superior feeling
Thinks schoolmates are all stupid
Too good for anybody
Thinks he (she) is always right
Thinks he (she) is the "greatest"
Thinks a lot of himself
Thinks he (she) is better than most
Thinks he (she) is "big deal"

Thinks he (she) is too smart
(to talk to)
Walks around with superior feeling
Makes fun of average students
Makes average students feel inferior
Snubs other people

TRAIT LIST II

Conscientious [a]
Ambitious
Has initiative
Has stick-to-itiveness
Hard working
Intent on doing work well and
completely
Industrious
Persevering
Willing to undertake a job
regardless of difficulty
Eager to take on new obligations
Cares about his (her) work
Enjoys his (her) studies
Studious [a]
Does not apply himself (herself)
to school work
Works hard to get high marks
Always wanting to learn

[a] Trait selected for the final trait list.

81

TRAIT LIST III

Doesn't have much to say
Hides feelings
Introvert
Mostly listening instead of talking
Not too talkative
Shy[a]
Quiet[a]
Talker
Talkative
Very forward

TRAIT LIST IV

Can't get a date[a]
Can't get along with other people
Doesn't mix well with other kids
Gets along with most anyone
Gets some dates
Gets lots of dates
Goes out with the popular boys
    (girls)
Has a hard time finding friends
Has few dates
Liked by all
Popular[a]
Not too much fun in a crowd
Not one of the gang
Shunned by others
Well-liked by fellow students
Wallflower

Doesn't go out with opposite sex
Disregards parties and clubs for his
    (her) work
Doesn't date much
Doesn't want to be in a gang
Doesn't care for opposite sex[a]
Doesn't have too many friends
Doesn't dance much
Easy to get along with
Easy to talk to
Friendly
Fun to be with
Hard to get along with
Likes people in general
Nice to everyone
Needs to help in human relations
Pleasant to be with
No one can get along with him (her)
Not sociable[a]
Stays at home a lot
Shy
Hardly ever goes to dances
Keeps to himself (herself)
Has his (her) own crowd
If you are not one of them you can't
    date them
Restricts friends to people on same
    intellectual scale
Sticks to his (her) own crowd[a]
Associates with people who are
    (also) very brilliant

Appendix B

Attitude Questionnaire

To All Students:

This is part of a survey of attitudes toward several types of high school students. The purpose of this questionnaire is to get your *opinions* on them. This is *not* a test in which there are right and wrong answers. Your judgment is as good as the next fellow's. We ask you to cooperate by honestly expressing your *true* opinions.

Before filling in the pages of the questionnaire please supply the information requested about your parents, and take the vocabulary quiz.

Date _____ Home Room Section _____

Name _____ School _____

Father's occupation _____

Father's education (please check all appropriate items):
_____ a) attended elementary school
_____ b) completed elementary school
_____ c) attended high school
_____ d) graduated from high school
_____ e) attended college
_____ f) graduated from college

Mother's occupation _____

Mother's education (please check all appropriate items):
_____ a) attended elementary school
_____ b) completed elementary school
_____ c) attended high school
_____ d) graduated from high school
_____ e) attended college
_____ f) graduated from college

On each of the following pages in this booklet you will find a short paragraph describing one type of high school student. Read the description carefully and then look at the words or phrases listed beneath it. You will find a YES and a NO next to each item. Circle the YES next to the word or phrase which you think *usually* characterizes the type of student described in the paragraph. Circle the NO next to the word or phrase which *does not usually* characterize the kind of student described in the paragraph.

83

DIRECTIONS: In each group below, select the numbered word or phrase that MOST NEARLY corresponds in meaning to the word at the head of that group, and put its NUMBER in the parentheses at the right.

1 space
  1 school
  2 noon
  3 captain
  4 room
  5 board...( )

2 lift
  1 sort out
  2 raise
  3 value
  4 enjoy
  5 fancy...( )

3 concern
  1 see clearly
  2 engage
  3 furnish
  4 disturb
  5 have to do with...( )

4 broaden
  1 efface
  2 make level
  3 elapse
  4 embroider
  5 widen...( )

5 blunt
  1 dull
  2 drowsy
  3 deaf
  4 doubtful
  5 ugly...( )

6 accustom
  1 disappoint
  2 customary
  3 encounter
  4 get used to
  5 business...( )

7 chirrup
  1 aspen
  2 joyful
  3 capsize
  4 chirp
  5 incite...( )

8 edible
  1 auspicious
  2 eligible
  3 fit to eat
  4 sagacious
  5 able to speak...( )

9 pack
  1 puissance
  2 remonstrance
  3 agreement
  4 skillet
  5 pressure...( )

10 solicitor
  1 lawyer
  2 chieftain
  3 watchman
  4 maggot
  5 constable...( )

11 allusion
  1 aria
  2 illusion
  3 eulogy
  4 dream
  5 reference...( )

12 caprice
  1 value
  2 a star
  3 grimace
  4 whim
  5 inducement...( )

13 animosity
  1 hatred
  2 animation
  3 disobedience
  4 diversity
  5 friendship...( )

14 emanate
  1 populate
  2 free
  3 prominent
  4 rival
  5 come...( )

15 madrigal
  1 song
  2 mountebank
  3 lunatic
  4 ribald
  5 sycophant...( )

16 cloistered
  1 miniature
  2 bunched
  3 arched
  4 malady
  5 secluded...( )

17 encomium
  1 repetition
  2 friend
  3 panegyric
  4 abrasion
  5 expulsion...( )

18 pristine
  1 flashing
  2 earlier
  3 primeval
  4 bound
  5 green...( )

19 tactility
  1 tangibility
  2 grace
  3 subtlety
  4 extensibility
  5 manageableness..

20 sedulous
  1 muddied
  2 sluggish
  3 stupid
  4 assiduous
  5 corrupting...( )

Pupil A is a *brilliant* high school student who is always among the *highest* in class in all academic subjects. Pupil A spends *more* time at home studying school subjects and doing homework than do most students. Pupil A *is* sports-minded and participates in *many* athletic activities at school.

DIRECTIONS: Circle the YES if the word or phrase *usually* characterizes a student like Pupil A. Circle the NO if the word or phrase *does not usually* characterize a student like Pupil A.

		Pupil A is				*Pupil A*
YES	NO	1. A good sport	YES	NO	32.	Has good manners
YES	NO	2. A perfectionist	YES	NO	33.	Has a pleasing
YES	NO	3. A teacher's pet				personality
YES	NO	4. A brain	YES	NO	34.	Has good study habits
YES	NO	5. A walking dictionary	YES	NO	35.	Has an open mind to
YES	NO	6. A good school citizen				all situations
YES	NO	7. A bookworm	YES	NO	36.	Has good ideas
YES	NO	8. A creep	YES	NO	37.	Has an answer for
YES	NO	9. A good conversa-				every question
		tionalist	YES	NO	38.	Has a well-rounded life
YES	NO	10. A good leader	YES	NO	39.	Takes criticism well
YES	NO	11. Spoiled	YES	NO	40.	Brags about his (her)
YES	NO	12. Serious				marks
YES	NO	13. Nervous	YES	NO	41.	Complains about
YES	NO	14. Competitive				never knowing enough
YES	NO	15. Proud of his (her)	YES	NO	42.	Dislikes kids who get
		school work				high marks
YES	NO	16. Conscientious	YES	NO	43.	Likes school
YES	NO	17. Dull	YES	NO	44.	Talks about you
YES	NO	18. Mature				behind your back
YES	NO	19. Cheerful	YES	NO	45.	Sticks with his (her)
YES	NO	20. Shy				own crowd
YES	NO	21. Kind	YES	NO	46.	Dresses well
YES	NO	22. Nice looking	YES	NO	47.	Wears glasses
YES	NO	23. Obedient	YES	NO	48.	Expresses himself
YES	NO	24. Thin				(herself) well
YES	NO	25. Stuck-up	YES	NO	49.	Is in many extracur-
YES	NO	26. Studious				ricular activities
YES	NO	27. Quiet	YES	NO	50.	Can take responsibility
YES	NO	28. Popular	YES	NO	51.	Believes in all school
YES	NO	29. Sociable				work and no play
YES	NO	30. Healthy	YES	NO	52.	Can't get a date
YES	NO	31. Bright	YES	NO	53.	Doesn't have much fun
			YES	NO	54.	Doesn't care for the

Check one:

Pupil A is most probably _____a boy
               _____a girl
               _____either one

opposite sex

Pupil B is an *average* student who receives *fair* grades in all academic subjects. Pupil B spends *no more* time at home studying school subjects and doing homework than do most students. Pupil B *is* sports-minded and participates in *many* athletic activities at school.

DIRECTIONS: Circle the YES if the word or phrase *usually* characterizes a student like Pupil B. Circle the NO if the word or phrase *does not usually* characterize a student like Pupil B.

Pupil B is

YES NO	1.	A good sport
YES NO	2.	A perfectionist
YES NO	3.	A teacher's pet
YES NO	4.	A brain
YES NO	5.	A walking dictionary
YES NO	6.	A good school citizen
YES NO	7.	A bookworm
YES NO	8.	A creep
YES NO	9.	A good conversationalist
YES NO	10.	A good leader
YES NO	11.	Spoiled
YES NO	12.	Serious
YES NO	13.	Nervous
YES NO	14.	Competitive
YES NO	15.	Proud of his (her) school work
YES NO	16.	Conscientious
YES NO	17.	Dull
YES NO	18.	Mature
YES NO	19.	Cheerful
YES NO	20.	Shy
YES NO	21.	Kind
YES NO	22.	Nice looking
YES NO	23.	Obedient
YES NO	24.	Thin
YES NO	25.	Stuck-up
YES NO	26.	Studious
YES NO	27.	Quiet
YES NO	28.	Popular
YES NO	29.	Sociable
YES NO	30.	Healthy
YES NO	31.	Bright

Pupil B

YES NO	32.	Has good manners
YES NO	33.	Has a pleasing personality
YES NO	34.	Has good study habits
YES NO	35.	Has an open mind to all situations
YES NO	36.	Has good ideas
YES NO	37.	Has an answer for every question
YES NO	38.	Has a well-rounded life
YES NO	39.	Takes criticism well
YES NO	40.	Brags about his (her) marks
YES NO	41.	Complains about never knowing enough
YES NO	42.	Dislikes kids who get high marks
YES NO	43.	Likes school
YES NO	44.	Talks about you behind your back
YES NO	45.	Sticks with his (her) own crowd
YES NO	46.	Dresses well
YES NO	47.	Wears glasses
YES NO	48.	Expresses himself (herself) well
YES NO	49.	Is in many extracurricular activities
YES NO	50.	Can take responsibility
YES NO	51.	Believes in all school work and no play
YES NO	52.	Can't get a date
YES NO	53.	Doesn't have much fun
YES NO	54.	Doesn't care for the opposite sex

Check one:

Pupil B is most probably _____a boy

_____a girl

_____either one

Pupil C is a *brilliant* high school student who is always among the *highest* in class in all academic subjects. Pupil C spends *no more* time at home studying school subjects and doing homework than do most students. Pupil C *is* sports-minded and participates in *many* athletic activities at school.

DIRECTIONS: Circle the YES if the word or phrase *usually* characterizes a student like Pupil C. Circle the NO if the word or phrase *does not usually* characterize a student like Pupil C.

Pupil C is

YES NO   1. A good sport
YES NO   2. A perfectionist
YES NO   3. A teacher's pet
YES NO   4. A brain
YES NO   5. A walking dictionary
YES NO   6. A good school citizen
YES NO   7. A bookworm
YES NO   8. A creep
YES NO   9. A good conversa-
             tionalist
YES NO   10. A good leader
YES NO   11. Spoiled
YES NO   12. Serious
YES NO   13. Nervous
YES NO   14. Competitive
YES NO   15. Proud of his (her)
             school work
YES NO   16. Conscientious
YES NO   17. Dull
YES NO   18. Mature
YES NO   19. Cheerful
YES NO   20. Shy
YES NO   21. Kind
YES NO   22. Nice looking
YES NO   23. Obedient
YES NO   24. Thin
YES NO   25. Stuck-up
YES NO   26. Studious
YES NO   27. Quiet
YES NO   28. Popular
YES NO   29. Sociable
YES NO   30. Healthy
YES NO   31. Bright

Pupil C

YES NO   32. Has good manners
YES NO   33. Has a pleasing
             personality
YES NO   34. Has good study habits
YES NO   35. Has an open mind to
             all situations
YES NO   36. Has good ideas
YES NO   37. Has an answer for
             every question
YES NO   38. Has a well-rounded life
YES NO   39. Takes criticism well
YES NO   40. Brags about his (her)
             marks
YES NO   41. Complains about
             never knowing enough
YES NO   42. Dislikes kids who get
             high marks
YES NO   43. Likes school
YES NO   44. Talks about you
             behind your back
YES NO   45. Sticks with his (her)
             own crowd
YES NO   46. Dresses well
YES NO   47. Wears glasses
YES NO   48. Expresses himself
             (herself) well
YES NO   49. Is in many extracur-
             ricular activities
YES NO   50. Can take responsibility
YES NO   51. Believes in all school
             work and no play
YES NO   52. Can't get a date
YES NO   53. Doesn't have much fun
YES NO   54. Doesn't care for the
             opposite sex

Check one:

Pupil C is most probably _____a boy
                         _____a girl
                         _____either one

Pupil D is an *average* student who receives *fair* grades in all academic subjects. Pupil D spends *more* time at home studying school subjects and doing homework than do most students. Pupil D *is* sports-minded and participates in *many* athletic activities at school.

DIRECTIONS: Circle the YES if the word or phrase *usually* characterizes a student like Pupil D. Circle the NO if the word or phrase *does not usually* characterize a student like Pupil D.

Pupil D is

YES NO   1. A good sport
YES NO   2. A perfectionist
YES NO   3. A teacher's pet
YES NO   4. A brain
YES NO   5. A walking dictionary
YES NO   6. A good school citizen
YES NO   7. A bookworm
YES NO   8. A creep
YES NO   9. A good conversationalist
YES NO 10. A good leader
YES NO 11. Spoiled
YES NO 12. Serious
YES NO 13. Nervous
YES NO 14. Competitive
YES NO 15. Proud of his (her) school work
YES NO 16. Conscientious
YES NO 17. Dull
YES NO 18. Mature
YES NO 19. Cheerful
YES NO 20. Shy
YES NO 21. Kind
YES NO 22. Nice looking
YES NO 23. Obedient
YES NO 24. Thin
YES NO 25. Stuck-up
YES NO 26. Studious
YES NO 27. Quiet
YES NO 28. Popular
YES NO 29. Sociable
YES NO 30. Healthy
YES NO 31. Bright

Pupil D

YES NO 32. Has good manners
YES NO 33. Has a pleasing personality
YES NO 34. Has good study habits
YES NO 35. Has an open mind to all situations
YES NO 36. Has good ideas
YES NO 37. Has an answer for every question
YES NO 38. Has a well-rounded life
YES NO 39. Takes criticism well
YES NO 40. Brags about his (her) marks
YES NO 41. Complains about never knowing enough
YES NO 42. Dislikes kids who get high marks
YES NO 43. Likes school
YES NO 44. Talks about you behind your back
YES NO 45. Sticks with his (her) own crowd
YES NO 46. Dresses well
YES NO 47. Wears glasses
YES NO 48. Expresses himself (herself) well
YES NO 49. Is in many extracurricular activities
YES NO 50. Can take responsibility
YES NO 51. Believes in all school work and no play
YES NO 52. Can't get a date
YES NO 53. Doesn't have much fun
YES NO 54. Doesn't care for the opposite sex

Check one:

Pupil D is most probably _____ a boy
_____ a girl
_____ either one

Pupil E is a *brilliant* high school student who is always among the *highest* in class in all academic subjects. Pupil E spends *no more* time at home studying school subjects and doing homework than do most students. Pupil E *is not* sports-minded and *does not* participate in many athletic activities at school.

DIRECTIONS: Circle the YES if the word or phrase *usually* characterizes a student like Pupil E. Circle the NO if the word or phrase *does not usually* characterize a student like Pupil E.

		Pupil E is			*Pupil E*
YES	NO	1. A good sport	YES	NO	32. Has good manners
YES	NO	2. A perfectionist	YES	NO	33. Has a pleasing personality
YES	NO	3. A teacher's pet			
YES	NO	4. A brain	YES	NO	34. Has good study habits
YES	NO	5. A walking dictionary	YES	NO	35. Has an open mind to all situations
YES	NO	6. A good school citizen			
YES	NO	7. A bookworm	YES	NO	36. Has good ideas
YES	NO	8. A creep	YES	NO	37. Has an answer for every question
YES	NO	9. A good conversationalist			
			YES	NO	38. Has a well-rounded life
YES	NO	10. A good leader	YES	NO	39. Takes criticism well
YES	NO	11. Spoiled	YES	NO	40. Brags about his (her) marks
YES	NO	12. Serious			
YES	NO	13. Nervous	YES	NO	41. Complains about never knowing enough
YES	NO	14. Competitive			
YES	NO	15. Proud of his (her) school work	YES	NO	42. Dislikes kids who get high marks
YES	NO	16. Conscientious	YES	NO	43. Likes school
YES	NO	17. Dull	YES	NO	44. Talks about you behind your back
YES	NO	18. Mature			
YES	NO	19. Cheerful	YES	NO	45. Sticks with his (her) own crowd
YES	NO	20. Shy			
YES	NO	21. Kind	YES	NO	46. Dresses well
YES	NO	22. Nice looking	YES	NO	47. Wears glasses
YES	NO	23. Obedient	YES	NO	48. Expresses himself (herself) well
YES	NO	24. Thin			
YES	NO	25. Stuck-up	YES	NO	49. Is in many extracurricular activities
YES	NO	26. Studious			
YES	NO	27. Quiet	YES	NO	50. Can take responsibility
YES	NO	28. Popular	YES	NO	51. Believes in all school work and no play
YES	NO	29. Sociable			
YES	NO	30. Healthy	YES	NO	52. Can't get a date
YES	NO	31. Bright	YES	NO	53. Doesn't have much fun
			YES	NO	54. Doesn't care for the opposite sex

Check one:

Pupil E is most probably _____a boy

_____a girl

_____either one

Pupil F is an *average* student who receives *fair* grades in all academic subjects. Pupil F spends *no more* time at home studying school subjects and doing homework than do most students. Pupil F *is not* sports-minded and *does not* participate in many athletic activities at school.

DIRECTIONS: Circle the YES if the word or phrase *usually* characterizes a student like Pupil F. Circle the NO if the word or phrase *does not usually* characterize a student like Pupil F.

Pupil F is

YES NO 1. A good sport
YES NO 2. A perfectionist
YES NO 3. A teacher's pet
YES NO 4. A brain
YES NO 5. A walking dictionary
YES NO 6. A good school citizen
YES NO 7. A bookworm
YES NO 8. A creep
YES NO 9. A good conversationalist
YES NO 10. A good leader
YES NO 11. Spoiled
YES NO 12. Serious
YES NO 13. Nervous
YES NO 14. Competitive
YES NO 15. Proud of his (her) school work
YES NO 16. Conscientious
YES NO 17. Dull
YES NO 18. Mature
YES NO 19. Cheerful
YES NO 20. Shy
YES NO 21. Kind
YES NO 22. Nice looking
YES NO 23. Obedient
YES NO 24. Thin
YES NO 25. Stuck-up
YES NO 26. Studious
YES NO 27. Quiet
YES NO 28. Popular
YES NO 29. Sociable
YES NO 30. Healthy
YES NO 31. Bright

Pupil F

YES NO 32. Has good manners
YES NO 33. Has a pleasing personality
YES NO 34. Has good study habits
YES NO 35. Has an open mind to all situations
YES NO 36. Has good ideas
YES NO 37. Has an answer for every question
YES NO 38. Has a well-rounded life
YES NO 39. Takes criticism well
YES NO 40. Brags about his (her) marks
YES NO 41. Complains about never knowing enough
YES NO 42. Dislikes kids who get high marks
YES NO 43. Likes school
YES NO 44. Talks about you behind your back
YES NO 45. Sticks with his (her) own crowd
YES NO 46. Dresses well
YES NO 47. Wears glasses
YES NO 48. Expresses himself (herself) well
YES NO 49. Is in many extracurricular activities
YES NO 50. Can take responsibility
YES NO 51. Believes in all school work and no play
YES NO 52. Can't get a date
YES NO 53. Doesn't have much fun
YES NO 54. Doesn't care for the opposite sex

Check one:
Pupil F is most probably ____a boy
____a girl
____either one

Pupil G is a *brilliant* high school student who is always among the *highest* in class in all academic subjects. Pupil G spends *more* time at home studying school subjects and doing homework than do most students. Pupil G *is not* sports-minded and *does not* participate in many athletic activities at school.

DIRECTIONS: Circle the YES if the word or phrase *usually* characterizes a student like Pupil G. Circle the NO if the word or phrase *does not usually* characterize a student like Pupil G.

		Pupil G is				*Pupil G*
YES	NO	1. A good sport	YES	NO	32.	Has good manners
YES	NO	2. A perfectionist	YES	NO	33.	Has a pleasing personality
YES	NO	3. A teacher's pet				
YES	NO	4. A brain	YES	NO	34.	Has good study habits
YES	NO	5. A walking dictionary	YES	NO	35.	Has an open mind to all situations
YES	NO	6. A good school citizen				
YES	NO	7. A bookworm	YES	NO	36.	Has good ideas
YES	NO	8. A creep	YES	NO	37.	Has an answer for every question
YES	NO	9. A good conversationalist	YES	NO	38.	Has a well-rounded life
YES	NO	10. A good leader	YES	NO	39.	Takes criticism well
YES	NO	11. Spoiled	YES	NO	40.	Brags about his (her) marks
YES	NO	12. Serious				
YES	NO	13. Nervous	YES	NO	41.	Complains about never knowing enough
YES	NO	14. Competitive				
YES	NO	15. Proud of his (her) school work	YES	NO	42.	Dislikes kids who get high marks
YES	NO	16. Conscientious	YES	NO	43.	Likes school
YES	NO	17. Dull	YES	NO	44.	Talks about you behind your back
YES	NO	18. Mature				
YES	NO	19. Cheerful	YES	NO	45.	Sticks with his (her) own crowd
YES	NO	20. Shy				
YES	NO	21. Kind	YES	NO	46.	Dresses well
YES	NO	22. Nice looking	YES	NO	47.	Wears glasses
YES	NO	23. Obedient	YES	NO	48.	Expresses himself (herself) well
YES	NO	24. Thin				
YES	NO	25. Stuck-up	YES	NO	49.	Is in many extracurricular activities
YES	NO	26. Studious				
YES	NO	27. Quiet	YES	NO	50.	Can take responsibility
YES	NO	28. Popular	YES	NO	51.	Believes in all school work and no play
YES	NO	29. Sociable				
YES	NO	30. Healthy	YES	NO	52.	Can't get a date
YES	NO	31. Bright	YES	NO	53.	Doesn't have much fun
			YES	NO	54.	Doesn't care for the opposite sex

Check one:

Pupil G is most probably _____a boy

_____a girl

_____either one

Pupil H is an *average* student who receives *fair* grades in all academic subjects. Pupil H spends *more* time at home studying school subjects and doing homework than do most students. Pupil H *is not* sports-minded and *does not* participate in many athletic activities at school.

DIRECTIONS: Circle the YES if the word or phrase *usually* characterizes a student like Pupil H. Circle the NO if the word or phrase *does not usually* characterize a student like Pupil H.

Pupil H is

YES NO	1.	A good sport
YES NO	2.	A perfectionist
YES NO	3.	A teacher's pet
YES NO	4.	A brain
YES NO	5.	A walking dictionary
YES NO	6.	A good school citizen
YES NO	7.	A bookworm
YES NO	8.	A creep
YES NO	9.	A good conversationalist
YES NO	10.	A good leader
YES NO	11.	Spoiled
YES NO	12.	Serious
YES NO	13.	Nervous
YES NO	14.	Competitive
YES NO	15.	Proud of his (her) school work
YES NO	16.	Conscientious
YES NO	17.	Dull
YES NO	18.	Mature
YES NO	19.	Cheerful
YES NO	20.	Shy
YES NO	21.	Kind
YES NO	22.	Nice looking
YES NO	23.	Obedient
YES NO	24.	Thin
YES NO	25.	Stuck-up
YES NO	26.	Studious
YES NO	27.	Quiet
YES NO	28.	Popular
YES NO	29.	Sociable
YES NO	30.	Healthy
YES NO	31.	Bright

Pupil H

YES NO	32.	Has good manners
YES NO	33.	Has a pleasing personality
YES NO	34.	Has good study habits
YES NO	35.	Has an open mind to all situations
YES NO	36.	Has good ideas
YES NO	37.	Has an answer for every question
YES NO	38.	Has a well-rounded life
YES NO	39.	Takes criticism well
YES NO	40.	Brags about his (her) marks
YES NO	41.	Complains about never knowing enough
YES NO	42.	Dislikes kids who get high marks
YES NO	43.	Likes school
YES NO	44.	Talks about you behind your back
YES NO	45.	Sticks with his (her) own crowd
YES NO	46.	Dresses well
YES NO	47.	Wears glasses
YES NO	48.	Expresses himself (herself) well
YES NO	49.	Is in many extracurricular activities
YES NO	50.	Can take responsibility
YES NO	51.	Believes in all school work and no play
YES NO	52.	Can't get a date
YES NO	53.	Doesn't have much fun
YES NO	54.	Doesn't care for the opposite sex

Check one:

Pupil H is most probably _____a boy

_____a girl

_____either one

Appendix C

Statistical Analyses of Student Reactions

TABLE 1: MEAN GLOBAL SCORES ASCRIBED TO EACH OF EIGHT STIMULUS CHARACTERS IN EACH OF EIGHT ORDERS, AND TOTAL ORDER AND STIMULUS CHARACTER MEANS AND STANDARD DEVIATIONS

(Total Population, N = 615)

Stimulus Character	Orders								Stimulus Character Mean	Standard Deviation
	1st	2d	3d	4th	5th	6th	7th	8th		
Brilliant-Nonstudious-Athletic	33.64	30.32	23.87	29.88	30.39	26.18	26.98	20.49	27.72	3.93
Average-Nonstudious-Athletic	32.95	29.55	25.83	28.09	28.92	22.27	23.54	19.74	26.36	3.87
Average-Studious-Athletic	29.73	25.60	24.71	14.90	29.59	22.49	21.20	21.48	23.71	4.55
Brilliant-Studious-Athletic	25.06	21.28	27.65	16.33	29.39	22.63	23.28	20.70	23.29	3.86
Brilliant-Nonstudious-Nonathletic	13.98	13.43	15.08	15.95	4.00	4.93	10.04	4.50	10.81	5.52
Average-Nonstudious-Nonathletic	12.09	22.33	8.68	13.75	2.67	5.47	11.50	10.00	10.24	4.75
Average-Studious-Nonathletic	2.23	14.74	12.82	13.46	2.63	8.34	1.72	7.48	7.93	5.01
Brilliant-Studious-Nonathletic	.23	3.09	4.93	4.60	2.03	2.53	4.31	-1.21	2.56	2.03
Order Mean	18.74	20.04	17.95	17.12	16.20	14.36	15.32	12.90		
Standard Deviation	12.58	8.61	8.12	7.68	13.39	9.23	9.02	8.26		

TABLE 1, *Continued*

ANALYSIS OF VARIANCE OF MEANS

	Sum of Squares	df	Mean Square	F
Total	6,481.09	63	102.87	
Stimulus Characters	5,283.62	7	754.73	39,843 [a]
Order	269.30	7	38.47	2,031 [b]
Interaction	928.17	49	18.94	

[a] Significant at or beyond the .05 level.
[b] Not significant.

TABLE 2: COMPARISONS OF THE MEAN GLOBAL SCORES FOR EACH STIMULUS CHARACTER ASCRIBED BY THE FEMALE AND MALE POPULATION

Stimulus Paragraph	$\overline{X}_F - \overline{X}_M$	t
Brilliant-Studious-Athletic	-.175	-.1309
Average-Nonstudious-Athletic	5.895	4.8598 [a]
Brilliant-Nonstudious-Athletic	6.086	4.9159 [a]
Average-Studious-Athletic	3.931	2.9735 [a]
Brilliant-Nonstudious-Nonathletic	5.029	3.3020 [a]
Average-Nonstudious-Nonathletic	.071	.0486
Brilliant-Studious-Nonathletic	-1.245	-.9841
Average-Studious-Nonathletic	.836	.5908

[a] Significant at or beyond the .05 level.

TABLE 3:   DIFFERENCES AMONG MEAN GLOBAL SCORES ASCRIBED TO THE EIGHT STIMULUS CHARACTERS
(Total Population, N = 615)

Stimulus Characters	Brilliant-Nonstudious-Athletic	Average-Nonstudious-Athletic	Average-Studious-Athletic	Brilliant-Studious-Athletic	Brilliant-Nonstudious-Nonathletic	Average-Nonstudious-Nonathletic	Average-Studious-Nonathletic	Brilliant-Studious-Nonathletic
Brilliant-Nonstudious-Athletic	—	2.24[a]	4.14[b]	4.60[b]	16.57[b]	17.70[b]	19.90[b]	26.15[b]
Average-Nonstudious-Athletic		—	1.91	2.37	14.34[b]	15.47[b]	17.67[b]	23.91[b]
Average-Studious-Athletic			—	.46	12.43[b]	13.56	15.76[b]	22.01[b]
Brilliant-Studious-Athletic				—	11.97[b]	13.10[b]	15.30[b]	21.55[b]
Brilliant-Nonstudious-Nonathletic					—	1.13	3.33	9.58[b]
Average-Nonstudious-Nonathletic						—	2.20	8.45[b]
Average-Studious-Nonathletic							—	6.25[b]
Brilliant-Studious-Nonathletic								—

[a] In all cases the difference is determined by subtracting the mean score for the stimulus character heading the column from the mean score for the stimulus character in the row to the left of the grid. In this instance +2.24 was derived by subtracting the mean score for Average-Nonstudious-Athletic (26.11) from the mean score for Brilliant-Nonstudious-Athletic (28.35).

[b] Significant at or beyond the .05 level.

TABLE 4: THREE-WAY ANALYSIS OF VARIANCE OF MEAN GLOBAL SCORES
ASCRIBED BY TOTAL POPULATION TO EIGHT STIMULUS CHARACTERS
(N=615 per cube)

Source of Variation	Sums of Squares	df	Variance Estimate	F
Average-Brilliant	856.67	1	856.67	3.05[a]
Nonstudious-Studious	25,719.51	1	25,719.51	91.61[b]
Athletic-Nonathletic	369,633.34	1	369,633.34	1,316.56[b]
Interaction: Ability and Effort	7,795.38	1	7,795.38	27.77[b]
Interaction: Ability and Athleticism	3,648.88	1	3,648.88	13.00[b]
Interaction: Effort and Athleticism	3,199.20	1	3,199.20	11.39[b]
Interaction: Ability and Effort and Athleticism	622.73	1	622.73	2.22[a]
Within group	1,379,077.83	4,912	280.76	
Total	1,790,553.53	4,919		

[a] Not significant.   [b] Significant at the .05 level or beyond.

TABLE 5: THREE-WAY ANALYSIS OF VARIANCE OF MEAN GLOBAL SCORES
ASCRIBED BY FEMALE POPULATION TO EIGHT STIMULUS CHARACTERS
(N=310 per cube)

Source of Variation	Sums of Squares	df	Variance Estimate	F
Brilliant-Average	560.50	1	560.50	2.14[a]
Studious-Nonstudious	24,513.39	1	24,513.39	93.41[b]
Athletic-Nonathletic	216,639.53	1	216,639.53	825.53[b]
Interaction: Ability and Effort	9,480.97	1	9,480.97	45.60[b]
Interaction: Ability and Athleticism	494.13	1	494.13	1.88[a]
Interaction: Effort and Athleticism	581.61	1	581.61	2.22[a]
Interaction: Ability and Effort and Athleticism	1,438.84	1	1,438.84	5.48[b]
Within group	648,718.73	2,472	262.43	
Total	902,427.71	2,479		

[a] Not significant.   [b] Significant at the .05 level or beyond.

TABLE 6:   THREE-WAY ANALYSIS OF VARIANCE OF MEAN GLOBAL SCORES
ASCRIBED BY MALE POPULATION TO EIGHT STIMULUS CHARACTERS
(N=305 per cube)

Source of Variation	Sums of Squares	df	Variance Estimate	F
Brilliant-Average	313.06	1	313.06	1.07 [a]
Studious-Nonstudious	4,883.73	1	4,883.73	16.66 [b]
Athletic-Nonathletic	155,297.20	1	155,297.20	529.84 [b]
Interaction: Ability and Effort	740.30	1	740.30	2.53 [a]
Interaction: Ability and Athleticism	4,025.12	1	4,025.12	13.70 [b]
Interaction: Effort and Athleticism	1,705.57	1	1,705.57	5.82 [b]
Interaction: Ability and Effort and Athleticism	400.03	1	400.03	1.37 [a]
Within group		2,432	293.11	
Total		2,439		

[a] Not significant.
[b] Significant at the .05 level or beyond.

TABLE 7: INTERCORRELATIONS AMONG SCORES ON DESIRABLE AND UNDESIRABLE TRAITS ASCRIBED TO THE EIGHT STIMULUS CHARACTERS

Stimulus Characters	Brilliant-Nonstudious-Athletic		Average-Nonstudious-Athletic		Average-Studious-Athletic		Brilliant-Studious-Athletic		Brilliant-Nonstudious-Nonathletic		Average-Nonstudious-Nonathletic		Average-Studious-Nonathletic		Brilliant-Studious-Nonathletic	
	Des.	Undes.	Des.	Undes.	Des.	Undes.	Des.	Undes.	Des.	Undes.	Des.	Undes.	Des.	Undes.	Des.	Undes.
Brilliant-Nonstudious-Athletic																
Desirable	—	-.527	.345	-.334	.378	-.154	.164	-.073	.233	-.076	.035	-.123	.041	-.019	.137	-.096
Undesirable		—	-.091	.292	-.154	.340	-.229	.303	-.090	.266	.055	.200	.022	.138	.014	.094
Average-Nonstudious-Athletic																
Desirable			—	-.461	.391	-.179	.285	-.011	.109	-.098	.212	-.005	.200	.008	.112	.101
Undesirable				—	-.199	.415	-.417	.283	-.023	.024	.049	.120	.008	.113	.011	-.023
Average-Studious-Athletic																
Desirable					—	-.536	.280	-.051	.175	-.080	.121	-.097	.185	-.044	.236	-.034
Undesirable						—	-.285	.232	-.114	.209	.048	.236	-.032	.192	-.134	.152
Brilliant-Studious-Athletic																
Desirable							—	-.536	.164	-.072	-.004	-.008	.105	-.058	.210	-.027
Undesirable								—	-.073	.275	.008	.110	-.092	.196	-.042	.239
Brilliant-Nonstudious-Nonathletic																
Desirable									—	-.552	.338	-.297	.305	-.069	.363	-.130
Undesirable										—	-.170	.357	-.103	.194	-.202	.385
Average-Nonstudious-Nonathletic																
Desirable											—	-.411	.481	-.144	.250	-.089
Undesirable												—	.223	.308	-.161	.106
Average-Studious-Nonathletic																
Desirable													—	-.447	.348	-.160
Undesirable														—	-.169	.269
Brilliant-Studious-Nonathletic																
Desirable															—	-.457
Undesirable																—

TABLE 8:   NUMBER OF MALE RESPONDENTS DESIGNATING EACH OF THE
EIGHT STIMULUS CHARACTERS AS "BOY," "GIRL," OR "EITHER"
(N=305)

Stimulus Characters	Boy	Girl	Either	Omit
Brilliant-Nonstudious-Athletic	142	36	100	27
Average-Nonstudious-Athletic	182	16	73	34
Average-Studious-Athletic	137	35	109	24
Brilliant-Studious-Athletic	154	28	91	32
Brilliant-Nonstudious-Nonathletic	125	44	104	32
Average-Nonstudious-Athletic	136	27	107	35
Average-Studious-Nonathletic	124	43	103	34
Brilliant-Studious-Nonathletic	110	59	104	32

TABLE 9:   NUMBER OF FEMALE RESPONDENTS DESIGNATING EACH OF THE
EIGHT STIMULUS CHARACTERS AS "BOY," "GIRL," OR "EITHER"
(N=310)

Stimulus Characters	Boy	Girl	Either	Omit
Brilliant-Nonstudious-Athletic	83	64	148	15
Average-Nonstudious-Athletic	103	35	136	36
Average-Studious-Athletic	80	49	157	24
Brilliant-Studious-Athletic	78	64	133	35
Brilliant-Nonstudious-Nonathletic	62	73	153	22
Average-Nonstudious-Nonathletic	73	66	155	16
Average-Studious-Nonathletic	58	74	150	28
Brilliant-Studious-Nonathletic	68	72	136	34

TABLE 10: CORRELATIONS BETWEEN RESPONDENTS' BACKGROUND FACTORS AND SCORES ON DESIRABLE TRAITS ASCRIBED TO THE STIMULUS CHARACTERS (Total Population, N=615)

Background Factor	Brilliant-Studious-Athletic	Average-Nonstudious-Athletic	Brilliant-Nonstudious-Athletic	Average-Studious-Athletic	Brilliant-Nonstudious-Nonathletic	Average-Nonstudious-Nonathletic	Brilliant-Studious-Nonathletic	Average-Studious-Nonathletic
Father's education	.022	.061	.061	.056	.013	−.013	−.012	.011
Mother's education	.067	.043	.072	.080	.031	−.013	.021	.072
Vocabulary score	.101	.000	.135	.063	.054	−.062	−.005	−.018

TABLE 11: CORRELATIONS BETWEEN RESPONDENTS' BACKGROUND FACTORS AND SCORES ON UNDESIRABLE TRAITS ASCRIBED TO THE STIMULUS CHARACTERS (Total Population, N=615)

Background Factor	Brilliant-Studious-Athletic	Average-Nonstudious-Athletic	Brilliant-Nonstudious-Athletic	Average-Studious-Athletic	Brilliant-Nonstudious-Nonathletic	Average-Nonstudious-Nonathletic	Brilliant-Studious-Nonathletic	Average-Studious-Nonathletic
Father's education	−.055	−.061	−.045	−.089	−.020	−.014	.007	.048
Mother's education	−.055	−.070	−.096	−.124	−.022	−.015	−.033	−.034
Vocabulary score	−.107	−.050	−.098	−.068	−.074	−.040	.026	−.022